Harry Houdini

Young Magician

Illustrated by Fred Irvin

Harry Houdini

Young Magician

By Kathryn Kilby Borland
and
Helen Ross Speicher

Aladdin Paperbacks

First Aladdin Paperbacks edition 1991
Copyright © 1969 by the Bobbs-Merrill Company, Inc.

ALADDIN PAPERBACKS
An imprint of Simon & Schuster Children's Publishing Division
1230 Avenue of the Americas, New York, NY 10020

Manufactured in the United States of America

26 28 30 29 27

Library of Congress Cataloging-in-Publication Data
Borland, Kathryn Kilby.
Harry Houdini : young magician / by Kathryn Kilby Borland and Helen Ross
Speicher: illustrated by Fred Irvin. —1st Aladdin Books ed.   p.   cm.
Reprint. Originally published under title: Harry Houdini, boy magician. 1969.
Summary: A biography of Harry Houdini concentrating on his earlier years
and the training that made him a master magician and escape artist.
1. Houdini, Harry, 1874–1926—Juvenile literature.
2. Magicians—United States—Biography—Juvenile literature.
[1. Houdini, Harry, 1874–1926. 2. Magicians.]
I. Speicher, Helen Ross. II. Irvin, Fred M., ill. III. Borland, Kathryn Kilby,
Harry Houdini, boy magician. IV. Title.
GV1545.H8B6   1991
793.8'092—dc20   [B] [92] 90-23321 CIP   AC
ISBN-13: 978-0-689-71476-4 (Aladdin pbk.)
ISBN-10: 0-689-71476-9 (Aladdin pbk.)

*To our children, all of whom
are escape artists of a different kind*

Illustrations

Full pages

Numerous smaller illustrations

Contents

★ ★

★ ★ # Harry
Houdini

Young Magician

A Bucket
of Coins

"WATCH CLOSELY," the magician on the platform was saying. "Watch me pick enough coins out of the air to fill the empty bucket."

He waved his hands to show that they were empty. He turned the bucket upside down to show that it was also empty. "If you can find out how I do it," he went on, "everyone in Appleton, Wisconsin, will be richer by nightfall."

Seven-year-old Ehrich Weiss moved closer to the platform. He had watched the man do the trick three times. It couldn't be as easy as it looked. The magician must be doing something special, but Ehrich couldn't find out what it was.

It had taken him most of the afternoon to see the trick that many times.

The magician did only a few tricks outside the sideshow tent. Then he went inside to do a longer show before he came out again. Of course the real show cost money, and Ehrich didn't have any. Not yet anyway, but when he discovered the coin trick, he would have all he needed.

His blue eyes grew larger and darker as he thought about taking the money home. Perhaps his mother would be sitting in the rocking chair in the kitchen darning socks. He would run into the room and empty the whole bucketful into her lap. Her beautiful dark eyes would shine, and she would say——

"Hey, kid!" the magician said, "why don't you go home like everybody else? You make me nervous watching, watching all day."

Ehrich looked around. It was true. He was the only one watching now. "I'm sorry, sir," he said. "I didn't think you'd notice me. It's just that I need to know how to fill the bucket with money, and I don't think I can quite do it yet. Could you—" Ehrich hesitated. Mysto had sounded pretty cross.

The magician stared at him. "Are you pulling my leg, kid? Do you think I really pull money out of the air?"

"You don't really?" Ehrich asked. He was so pleased that the magician was actually talking to him that he almost forgot to be disappointed about not taking a bucket of money home. "Then where did it come from?"

Suddenly the magician smiled. "Look here, kid," he said. "I'm going to show you something. It's not what you really do in this business that counts. It's what people think you do. Now, when I show the empty bucket I hold it in my left hand, see? And in my left hand I also have a bunch of coins that nobody sees. They're too busy looking at the empty bucket. Now, in my right hand I have just one coin. See?"

Ehrich nodded. "But I saw you pick the coins out of the air."

"Aha! That's what you thought you saw. Here's what you really saw."

The man showed Ehrich that he was holding the coin behind his hand between his thumb and first finger. When he held his hand up, the coin did not show at all. Then he moved his fingers quickly. Now the coin could be plainly seen. Even though Ehrich saw him do the trick, it was hard to believe the man hadn't picked that coin out of the air.

"But how do you get another one after you throw that one in the bucket?"

"I don't throw it in."

"But I saw you do it every time."

"You thought you saw me. I acted as if I was throwing it in, but I slipped it in back of my hand again. At the same time I slipped a coin into the bucket out of my other hand. See how it's done? Come on up and try it."

"I don't think I could." But Ehrich's fingers were itching to try. He'd forgotten everything except the magician, the bucket, and the coins.

The first time he tried it the coins in his left hand fell to the floor. It was a hot day, and the coin in his right hand stuck between his fingers. He made every kind of mistake, but at last the magician said, "You're not doing badly, kid. You've got the fingers for it."

"Ehrich! What are you doing here?"

It was his father's voice. Suddenly Ehrich was back in the world of parents, dinner time, and papers which he hadn't sold.

"This is your father?" the magician asked.

"Yes, sir, it is," Ehrich answered. "This is my father, Dr. Weiss."

"Oh, your father's a doctor?"

"No, sir. My father is not a doctor. He is a rabbi," Ehrich said proudly.

The magician looked nervously at the small man in the shabby black suit. "I didn't mean any harm, sir," he said. "I was just teaching the boy a trick. He's pretty good at it, too. He has the hands for it."

Rabbi Weiss did not smile, but his voice was kind. "It was good of you to take the time. But we worry because we do not know where Ehrich is. And now we must hurry."

As they walked quickly through the circus grounds, Rabbi Weiss asked sadly, "Ehrich, do you not even know what day it is?"

Ehrich's face fell. "The eve of the Sabbath, Papa. I forgot."

"Yes, this is the eve of the Sabbath. We must hurry home before sunset. Never has everyone not been home when your mama lighted the Sabbath candles."

"Let's hurry, Papa," Ehrich urged. "I would not want not to be there."

Just outside the circus grounds Rabbi Weiss halted. "This sign," he said sternly.

"Yes, Papa?"

"This sign says 'Jack Hoeffler's Five-Cent Circus.' From where did you get the five cents to enter the circus grounds?"

"Well, Papa, the boys said—we—thought it would be all right—" Ehrich hesitated. His face was red, and he ended quickly, "I slipped under the ropes, Papa."

Rabbi Weiss frowned. "Does the sign say 'Five cents to everyone but Ehrich Weiss'? Tomorrow you will bring to this Mr. Hoeffler the five cents and beg his pardon."

Ehrich knew it was no use to argue with his father, but there were not many five-cent pieces to spare in the Weiss household. Dr. Weiss had brought his family to America from Hungary just before Ehrich was born. His wife's cousin had helped them to settle in Appleton.

There were not many Jewish people here in this small Wisconsin town in 1881, so there was not much demand for a rabbi to teach Hebrew. Dr. Weiss had been a respected scholar in Hungary. He could also teach French and German, but it seemed as if no one in Appleton wished to learn these languages either.

Ehrich had three brothers, and he knew it was a constant struggle to buy food and milk and shoes for all of them. But their mother managed well. They were never hungry, and they were always neat. The children worked as much as they were able. Even seven-year-old Ehrich sold newspapers and shined shoes. "Bit by bit the plate is filled," Mama often said.

"Hurry, Papa," Ehrich urged as they turned the corner to the street where they lived. Their house needed paint, and it was too small, but

Ehrich knew that inside there would be the special feeling and the lovely smell of Sabbath Eve. All kinds of smells made up this odor. There was the delicate herb odor of good cooking, the richer odor of chicken fat, and even the wet smell of freshly scrubbed floors.

His mother was standing in the doorway. "Ehrich, what happened to you? You are so dirty for the Sabbath. And to make Papa come for you when he was already so tired."

"I'm sorry, Mama."

"What was worse was that the other boys had to sell your papers because you forgot," Dr. Weiss said. "And Mama has been worried because you forgot. And why? Because of some great event? Because of some emergency? No, because of a worthless magic show."

"But Papa——"

Mrs. Weiss spoke quickly. "Ehrich, you must wash right now as best you can. There is no

19

time for you to change your clothes. It is time to light the candles."

Ehrich splashed about briefly in the kitchen washbowl. His face and hands were spotless when he came to the table. There wouldn't be time for his mother to inspect his neck and ears.

The table was spread with the fine white linen cloth Mrs. Weiss had brought with her from Hungary. In the center of the table was the heavy silver candelabra which had belonged to the family for many years.

His mother lighted the tall tapers. "May our home be consecrated, O God, by Thy light," she said as they bowed their heads.

Ehrich looked around him. It seemed as if everyone looked different and better at the Sabbath Eve table. His older brothers sat at one end and Ehrich and his younger brother, Dash, sat at the other side. They were the same brothers who teased each other and sometimes fought

during the week, but now they looked as if they never would. It was more than just having clean hands and wearing their best clothes. There was something special about Sabbath Eve.

Ehrich suddenly realized that he was hungry. While his father was blessing the food, Ehrich could smell the chicken and dumplings waiting for them in the kitchen. The challas, the braided Sabbath bread, was almost under his nose. If his father said another word he would have to break off a piece and cram it into his mouth. At last his father finished the blessing, and his mother brought in the chicken, shining under its rich yellow coat of gravy.

One thing was lucky for Ehrich. His father always asked questions at this meal. He asked about the Torah and Jewish history. Everyone would be so busy they wouldn't have time to ask what he had been doing at the circus. If he talked about it he'd be almost sure to tell them that he'd made up his mind that afternoon to be a magician. If he told them, they'd laugh at him, and he didn't want to be laughed at.

He'd heard his father say that nothing was impossible if you wanted to do it badly enough and were willing to work for it. He'd never wanted anything so badly as to stand on a platform and do impossible things while everyone applauded. He was willing to work hard to do it. And the magician had said he had the fingers for it.

Ehrich, Prince
of the Air

"WATCH ME. I'm going to pick up these pins with my eyelids." Nine-year-old Ehrich was hanging by his knees from a low trapeze. In the tent of Jack Hoeffler's Five-Cent Circus two men looked at the boy.

"No, I couldn't use that act," Mr. Hoeffler said impatiently. "Only the people in the front row could see what you're doing."

"Oh, but I do other things, sir." Ehrich flipped easily down from the trapeze to stand in front of the circus owner.

It was good to have his feet on circus sawdust again. Last summer he had spent every possible

24

moment with both of the traveling circuses which had come to Appleton.

"I can climb higher and jump farther than any other boy in town," he insisted. "And I can balance on top of anything you name."

Mr. Hoeffler looked more closely at the short, broad-shouldered boy standing so cockily in front of him. "You're sure you're not afraid of high places?" he asked.

"Sure I'm sure," Ehrich answered. "I'm Ehrich, Prince of the Air."

Mr. Hoeffler laughed. It might not be such a bad idea to hire a local boy. It might even be good for business. After all, he'd have to stay in Appleton until the broken wheel of the animal wagon was fixed. That might take a week.

"All right," he said at last. "I'll hire you for this next week."

Ehrich's back straightened. "Thank you, sir. You'll be glad you did. I'll work hard."

Leaving the tent, Mr. Hoeffler said, "Let's go talk to Zansu, the wire walker. Maybe you can help him with his ropes."

Ehrich's eyes were wide with excitement. Helper to a wire walker! He could help Papa buy food for the table. Perhaps he would be famous soon. Then he could bring that bucket of money home to Mama. Soon he would——

"Watch it, boy!" A loud voice made him jump back from a handsome, prancing white horse. The groom laughed and braided another pink paper rose into its mane.

Even the air was different in a circus. The smell of animals and canvas, sawdust and grease-paint was unlike any other. There were colors here seen nowhere else. Scarlet capes glittered with silver sequins. Black tights glowed with gold spangles.

Everywhere the circus people hurried about their jobs. Big-muscled men swung sledge hammers to make the tent stakes firm. Off to one side the three-man brass band was playing loudly and drawing a crowd already. A white-faced clown reddened his round nose as he peered into a mirror. A dwarf, barely two feet tall, held the mirror at the right angle.

Ehrich's eyes grew larger and larger trying to watch everything at once. He remembered seeing some of the circus people last summer.

They stopped by a slender Oriental man. Ehrich recognized this performer. Now he was carefully coiling some ropes and laying them in a small brass-bound trunk.

"This is your new helper, Zansu."

"So?" Zansu smiled down at Ehrich.

"Yes, sir," the boy said proudly. "I'm Ehrich, Prince of the Air."

"Good," the acrobat answered kindly. "Prince Ehrich may learn much from Zansu."

Zansu liked Ehrich. He even worked with

him patiently until he could do a short rope
walking act. It was a low rope, but the applause
from the audience seemed very loud to Ehrich.
He did a few easy magic tricks with handker-

chiefs in the sideshow, too. These needed more practice, but his audience was made up of neighbors and friends, and they were proud of him.

Every day he learned something new. He watched the magician whenever he could. He tried to imitate every move the man made over and over again. He learned that a good magician's tongue works as fast as his hands.

He watched the rope men as they made different kinds of knots. The tent ropes were not tied in the same way as Zansu's tight ropes. Some of the knots untied at a single pull. Others would hold up a grown man as he walked on the ropes, high in the air.

"Teach me how to tie that knot, please," Ehrich asked often.

"Watch fast, then. I don't have all day," was the usual answer. So Ehrich learned to watch closely the first time anything was explained to him. He might not have another chance.

29

"Why don't you ever rest, Zansu?" Ehrich asked one hot afternoon. "There's only an hour till the evening performance."

"I wish to become so good an acrobat that some day I may be hired by a first-rate circus," Zansu answered.

"But isn't Mr. Hoeffler's circus the best one?" Ehrich wondered.

"No, no, Ehrich." Zansu smiled at the question. "This is only a small three-wagon circus. I wish to go with a circus that needs forty wagons and has twelve elephants to pull them out of the spring mud. Some day I shall be good enough for that." Zansu leaped easily to the low practice rope. He did not seem to be tired. So Zansu dreamed of an even larger audience.

"Someday I will entertain an audience that stops cracking peanut shells just to watch me," Ehrich said. "I will make my show so exciting that people will forget everything else."

"I could give you your chance, boy," Mr. Hoeffler's voice boomed out in back of Ehrich. "The circus is leaving tonight after the evening show. Zansu says he could use you. But I don't suppose you could go with us?" Mr. Hoeffler looked steadily at Ehrich.

Ehrich felt his throat tighten. Could he leave Appleton tonight? What would Papa and Mama say? But Mr. Hoeffler and Zansu really wanted him to go with them. He wanted to be a showman, and this was his big chance to earn money the family needed. Mama said often enough that luck alone does not help a man if a man does not help it along. Well, wasn't this his chance to help it along?

That night the flaring torches shone more brightly than ever before. The bareback rider on the white horse sparkled more brilliantly in her pink tights. The white-faced clown and the dwarf were simply hilarious. Zansu walked the

31

high wire so expertly that he seemed to touch the top of the tent. The magician had a new trick with three bright orange silk handkerchiefs. Even Ehrich had never received such loud applause before.

He looked for Papa and Mama, but the crowd was too large for him to see them until after the show was over. He was glad Papa had at last used the pass Mr. Hoeffler had given him. But what could he possibly say to make Papa understand that he had to go with the circus?

When he finally saw Papa and Mama outside the tent he didn't say the right thing at all. He just blurted out, "I am going to miss you when I leave Appleton."

"Leave Appleton?" Rabbi Weiss asked. "What does this mean, leave?"

"Mr. Hoeffler will pay me to travel with his circus," Ehrich explained. "I could send money home to you every week."

32

Rabbi Weiss exchanged a look with his wife. He cleared his throat. "This you cannot do," he said quietly.

"But Papa, it's my chance to help. The next circus may not hire me."

"A boy your age still needs his Mama," Mrs. Weiss said softly, her eyes shining with proud tears. "You can help us later."

Ehrich might have known it would be this way. "But Mr. Hoeffler expects me to go with him," he protested weakly.

"I will explain to him," his father said.

Suddenly Ehrich was furious. Why couldn't they understand? Already he was Ehrich, Prince of the Air. Soon, with a little practice, he could also be the greatest magician ever. Audiences from as far away as Milwaukee would come just to see him perform. He had to go.

Dash pulled at his sleeve. "Ehrich, you were the best one in the circus. Will you teach me how to walk the tightrope tomorrow?" Tomorrow, Ehrich thought, still in Appleton. The sudden anger left him. He put his arm around his little brother's shoulders.

"Tomorrow I'll bake for you some of your favorite bread," Mama promised. Bread for me, Ehrich thought, when I could be earning money to buy it for them.

"Thank you, Mama," he said sadly. "I'll get my things and come home with you." But I won't stop practicing, he promised himself fiercely. Someday I'll be so good the biggest circus will beg me to join it. My picture will be on all the billboards. Millions of people will——

"Ehrich," Papa said gently, "Mama is telling you she will bake the bread tonight if it will make you happier."

"Tomorrow will be fine, thank you, Mama." My tomorrow will come some day, Ehrich promised himself. I'll make it come.

The Terrible
Dr. Lynn

"You can do better than that, Dash. Tie me tight enough to make it hard." Ehrich handed the frayed rope to Dash.

Dash was tired of this chore. "I wish George White had never told you about the show in Minneapolis where the man escaped from the ropes," he said impatiently. "I can't help it if you can untie knots faster than I can tie them. I tied twelve knots in that rope."

"It isn't how many knots you tie," Ehrich said, "it's what kind. It's harder to get out of a rope tied with two or three good knots than with a dozen poor knots. The more you tie, the sloppier the last ones are. Here, let me show you some real knots."

Dash started to say he was ready to quit, but he decided it wasn't any use. If Ehrich made up his mind to do something he did it, no matter what anybody else thought.

Ehrich looped the rope around Dash several times and tied it with three tight knots. "Let's see you get out of that," he said.

"Of course I can't," Dash said. "I didn't say I could. I can't even get out of the easy ones, and I don't care."

"Well, try," Ehrich urged. "Nobody ever did anything they thought they couldn't do."

"Ehrich!" It was Mama's voice.

"Untie me before you go," Dash pleaded. But Ehrich was already halfway to the house.

His mother was standing in the kitchen doorway smiling. "Ehrich, Papa has a nice surprise for you," she said.

36

Papa came into the kitchen, carrying a book as always. He smiled too when he saw Ehrich. "Ah, Ehrich, you were so disappointed when the circus had to leave without you. I have wished to do something to make you happy. How would you like to take a trip with me?"

"Take a trip with you, Papa?" Ehrich stared at his father. He seldom went even into Appleton. "Where are we going, Papa?"

Dr. Weiss waited dramatically for a moment before answering. "We will go to Milwaukee next week." He was still looking at Ehrich.

Milwaukee? Papa never teased. It had to be so, but none of the family had been to Milwaukee. They had no money to go on trips. "We're going to Milwaukee, Papa? Truly?"

"Truly, my son. The daughter of Mr. Wolf is to be married in Milwaukee, and I am to perform the ceremony. Mr. Wolf said there would be room in the carriage for one boy. Because

37

you tried well to forget about the circus, Mama and I have decided that you should go."

"Oh, thank you, Papa. Thank you!" Ehrich began turning cartwheels over and over in the center of the big kitchen.

"Stop, Ehrich," his mother laughed. "Your father will not take you to Milwaukee with a broken leg. If you are so full of energy, you may peel some apples for the torte." Always when Mama was excited she talked very fast.

"Yes, Mama." Ehrich peeled six apples before he remembered Dash, tied up in the backyard.

Dash was red-faced and angry. "You just wait till I tell Papa what you did."

Ehrich was horrified. "Oh no. Dash, please don't tell," he begged. His father would certainly not take him to Milwaukee if Dash told. But Dash looked angrier every minute. Ehrich untied him as slowly as possible. He knew the minute Dash was free he would hurry to find Papa. "Listen, Dash, I'll give you all my marbles if you won't tell." Dash shook his head.

"My pocket knife?" Ehrich asked slowly, almost hoping Dash wouldn't take it.

"What's the reason you don't want me to tell?" Dash asked, looking at his brother shrewdly. "I don't want your marbles or your knife, but I'll tell you what. If you'll show me how to put the coins in the bucket, I won't tell."

Ehrich would never show anyone the secrets of any of the tricks he could do, if he could help it. But he didn't know when he'd ever have another chance to go to Milwaukee.

"All right," he said, "go and get a bucket and some pebbles to use for coins." He'd much rather Dash had taken his knife.

The trip in Mr. Wolf's carriage had been exciting. Ehrich tried to look in every direction at once. After the marriage there had been a wonderful dinner. But none of that was important compared to what happened next.

"Rabbi," Mr. Wolf said, "before we go back to Appleton I have a little business at the bank. While I am busy I would like for you and Ehrich to be my guests at the theater. A magician is playing there. He's said to be good."

"Ehrich and I can walk about the city," Dr. Weiss said. "There is no need for you to entertain us." Then he looked at Ehrich and added quickly, "But since you are so kind, perhaps it would be pleasant."

"I would have died if you had said no, Papa," Ehrich told his father when they were alone.

"Probably few people have died from not seeing magicians," his father answered. "But I am happy that we did not take that chance."

The theater was more magnificent than Ehrich could have imagined. There were acres of red plush seats. The stage was hidden by a red velvet curtain which hung in rich-looking folds. Ehrich and his father were almost the first ones in the theater. Their seats were only a few rows from the stage.

When the lights went off and the velvet curtains began to open slowly, Ehrich thought this must surely be the most exciting moment in the world. Then he forgot that he was Ehrich Weiss, forgot that his father was beside him, forgot that he was in Milwaukee. He saw only the tall, dark-haired man who was standing on the stage. The playbills outside the theater had said that he was Dr. Lynn.

First Dr. Lynn pulled yards and yards of different colored silks from an empty vase. He brought two pigeons out of a perfectly ordinary hat. He borrowed a watch from a gentleman in the audience and smashed it to bits with a hammer. Then he shook the bits up in a handkerchief. When he shook out the handkerchief, there was the watch, whole and shining. Mysto's tricks had been small and ordinary next to the tricks of this magician.

Dr. Lynn stepped to the front of the stage. "Now," he said, "I will produce for you one of my greatest illusions."

Ehrich nudged his father. "What's an illusion?" he whispered.

"An illusion looks like something it is not," Rabbi Weiss explained.

Ehrich nodded. "I see," he said, although he really didn't understand.

"First," Dr. Lynn was saying, "I must ask for absolute silence. This is a very dangerous trick. If my hand should slip, my assistant would be in the utmost peril."

Ehrich shivered. He liked the scary sound of those words—*utmost peril*.

A small worried-looking man edged his way out onto the stage. He and Dr. Lynn shook hands. "This is a fearless man," Dr. Lynn said. Ehrich thought the man did not look too fearless. Two pretty ladies rolled out a small table on wheels. They strapped the man down.

Dr. Lynn pulled on a pair of rubber gloves. "Chloroform!" he called. One lady handed him a large green bottle and a handkerchief. "This is an operation," Dr. Lynn explained to the audience, "and it is better for the patient to be unconscious. Otherwise he might scream, and that would make my hand shake."

The doctor poured liquid out of the bottle over the handkerchief and held it over the man's nose. Ehrich sat on the edge of his seat. He was sure he could smell the awful chloroform. Dr. Lynn held up his hand for silence. He raised one of the man's eyelids and looked into his eyes. Then he held his wrist for a moment.

"I am ready," he announced. One of the ladies handed him an enormous saw. He tested its edge

43

with his thumb and nodded. Then, walking over to the table, he held the saw over the leg of the unconscious man.

Ehrich gasped as Dr. Lynn began sawing. Why didn't somebody stop him? But it was too late. The terrible Dr. Lynn was handing the man's leg to his helper. "Take care of this. We will need it later," he said calmly.

Ehrich looked at his father, but his father was smiling—his father who had once stopped some boys on the street and scolded them for pulling the wings off a butterfly.

Dr. Lynn cut off the man's other leg and both arms. Each time someone in the audience screamed. Then Dr. Lynn covered the pieces with a blanket. He waved his arms over it and spoke some long words. One of the ladies removed the blanket. The man jumped from the table, bowed, and waved with two perfectly good arms.

The audience clapped and cheered. Ehrich wondered how it would feel to be Dr. Lynn—to be able to make an audience laugh or scream or almost stop breathing. It might be even better than being a circus performer.

He hardly said a word all the way back to Appleton. "He's asleep," Dr. Weiss told Mr. Wolf. "It has been a busy day."

But Ehrich wasn't asleep. He was remembering what Mysto had told him. "It isn't what you do. It's what people think you do." He was trying to see again every move Dr. Lynn had made so he would know what the magician had really done.

A Promise
to Keep

"Mama, where are you?" Ehrich's voice rang through the dark little house.

"I am washing the kitchen floor. Poverty may come from God, but not dirt."

"Oh, Mama, look! I have found a new kind of lock." Ehrich held out the metal.

"Another lock? As welcome as water in a leaking ship," Mrs. Weiss replied calmly.

Ehrich was always bringing home strange fastenings from the Appleton dump. Locks of any kind or shape on trunks or doors or chests enchanted him. Each new one had to be opened. Each part had to be examined.

"But I've never seen one like this before," Ehrich explained. "I've got to take it apart to see how it works." Ehrich was as happy as a puppy with two tails.

"This is something new to do?" Mrs. Weiss asked. But Ehrich was already taking the lock apart with a screwdriver.

Since his eleventh birthday he had divided his interest between locks and magic. Locks had won the lion's share of his time. Books on magic were too expensive to buy. There were never any extra pennies to spend on gay colored silks or stiff new decks of cards. Magic acts had to be conjured simply with the aid of the Weiss pots and pans. Ehrich had no clear crystal bowls or beautiful artificial flowers.

Ehrich visited the junkyards regularly. Once in a great while he brought home a treasure, like the day he found an old discolored nickel in a shabby leather purse. Mostly, though, he turned up only parts which had to be worked into something else. He had made a toy for Dash from three wheels and some old boards.

"Dash," Ehrich called now, "come see my new lock. It's a different kind." He could hear Dash thumping on the hall floor.

"Just a minute." Dash sounded breathless. "I'm trying to beat your somersault record."

"You'll never do that," Ehrich laughed. "If you do, I'll just turn an extra twenty."

"Yes, I suppose you would." Dash opened the hall door, red-faced and breathing hard. He was taller than his older brother already, but not so broad-shouldered. "No matter how hard I try, you always do things better than I do. I'll never be able to beat you." He wiped his wet forehead on his dusty sleeve.

"It's because I work harder at it," Ehrich said. "You exercise just when you feel like it, but I do it every day. I get up an hour before you do and spend the whole time doing exercises. Mama would say——"

"I know. Mama would say 'He who sleeps late has a short day.' But if it depends on giving up any sleep, I'll always be second best."

"That's where we're different. I will never be second best." Then, seeing Dash's face, Ehrich added, "But you were pretty good at getting loose yesterday."

"That's because we were playing a game yesterday," Dash explained. "It was fun instead of work. Anyway, you didn't tie me up very tight. I made forty knots when I tied you, and you were loose before I could get out of sight."

"Tying forty knots doesn't have anything to do with it. I've told you a hundred times that it's not the knots that are important. It's how much slack you leave in the rope."

A scanty dinner that night left Ehrich wishing for more to eat. After dinner, Rabbi Weiss said,

"Ehrich, the locksmith tells me you give much time to his shop."

"Yes, Papa. You know how I like locks."

"He also tells me this. He will give you a job, which will help him and us." Rabbi Weiss did not look at his wife.

Ehrich knew how sad his father was because he could not earn enough for his family. He spoke quickly. "I could start right after school tomorrow, Papa. It will be an easy job."

He wished the locksmith could pay him enough so he could buy big heavy books for Papa and fine dresses for Mama. Someday, when he was performing in a circus or on the stage like Dr. Lynn, he would be very rich and would do all these things. "Ehrich the Great" he would call himself, and Papa and Mama would never need to worry about money again.

Within two weeks Ehrich had learned how every lock in the shop worked. Often it was dark before he left the locksmith's, but he always came home whistling happily.

One evening he began eagerly, "Mama, today I opened a lock on Mrs. White's attic trunk that had been stuck for over a year."

"Need sharpens the brain, my son."

"And Mama," he went on, "the best is not yet told. The locksmith gave me a whole quarter because I did it so quickly. Here it is, Mama. I give it to you."

"Oh, Ehrich! But it must go to Papa."

"Whatever pleases you, Mama." Ehrich felt good right down to his heels.

One hot summer day the sheriff of Appleton walked into the locksmith's shop. He was pushing a huge prisoner in front of him.

"Jim," the sheriff said, looking sheepish, "can you file off these handcuffs? I've lost the key. The judge says I've got to let him go. He says there's not enough evidence."

"I'll say there isn't." The prisoner glared. "Hurry it up!"

The locksmith laughed. "Beats all how you can lose things, Carl. Here, let me get at those iron bracelets."

The metal was hard, and the afternoon grew warmer. Sweat was streaming down the locksmith's face and neck. The prisoner growled impatiently as the file rasped on the cuffs.

Finally the sheriff said, "Jim, why don't you rest a spell? Let Ehrich earn his pay."

"Good idea," the locksmith agreed. "I'm sure tired of this job. Ehrich, come here and work on these pesky things for a while."

Ehrich began to rub the file across the rusty metal. The two men stretched out under the shade of the big apple tree in the yard.

Now Ehrich was alone with the prisoner. He felt the man's angry eyes glaring at him. He wished the prisoner wasn't so big. He could have been the giant in a sideshow. Ehrich kept on filing, but the iron didn't yield.

"Hurry up, can't you?" the big man grumbled.

"Maybe I'd better try something else," Ehrich answered, trying to look calm.

54

He felt around in his pocket. His slim fingers rejected tangles of string, a chipped marble, a rusty hinge, and two nails. Finally he pulled out a thin, straight piece of metal. This was his pride —a picklock which he had made to open locks which had no keys. It had opened Mama's cake cupboard at home more times than Mrs. Weiss realized.

Ehrich was glad the prisoner didn't seem to be interested in the little bit of thin wire. He opened the handcuffs carefully and stepped back quickly. He didn't know what the big man might do. He might even try to steal his picklock. It would be pretty handy if he was the kind of man who was arrested very often.

Ehrich stayed as far away from the man as he could in the small room. But the man only muttered, "Thanks, boy," before he hurried out the door. Ehrich gave a deep sigh of relief. His picklock was safe. The man had showed no interest in it. Ehrich jammed it back into his pocket. He had work to do.

That winter the locksmith moved to another town and Ehrich lost the job he liked so well. Of course he was busy. He sold newspapers. He blacked boots for businessmen. He chopped wood for stoves and fireplaces. He delivered packages for the grocery store. But all these jobs took time and paid very little. Each year the family became a little poorer, and now there was a new baby sister, Gladys.

Ehrich hated to see his parents look so tired. His older brothers had left home and were on their own now. Ehrich worked as hard as he could, but every day he was more convinced that he would never be able to help enough here in Appleton. He might even have to leave home some day.

On his twelfth birthday his father called him. Rabbi Weiss looked tired and sad. "Ehrich," he began, "come with me. I must have a serious talk with you."

"Yes, Papa?" Ehrich tried to stand taller.

"Work is no longer easy for me. I am getting much older. You must make me a promise."

"Of course I will, Papa." Ehrich wondered what it could be.

"You of all the children show the most love for your mother. Promise me that you will always see that she is taken care of."

"Oh yes, Papa," Ehrich promised eagerly, "I will." Ehrich knew that Papa was twenty-five years older than Mama. It had been a long time since he was a young man.

"Never forget this. I must trust in you."

Ehrich shivered as he watched his father leave the room. How slowly he walked. "Now I will have to leave home to keep my promise to Papa," Ehrich told himself solemnly.

Your Truant
Son, Ehrich

EHRICH shut the back door quietly behind him. It was going to be a beautiful April day, even if it was chilly. The sun was bright, and it would be warm by afternoon.

He walked slowly through the neat little backyard. What would everyone say when he didn't come to breakfast? He could imagine the hurt look in Papa's and Mama's eyes. Of course he could turn back. It wasn't too late.

But all this last year he had kept remembering his promise to his father. He was sure now that he could never earn much here in Appleton. He wasn't clever in school. He could never become a scholar. It took money to be a scholar anyway. He didn't want to be an errand boy all his life—a shoeshiner, a newspaper seller. Of course he wanted to send money home to his family, but he wanted even more than that. He wanted to stand on a stage like Dr. Lynn and Mysto. He wanted to be famous.

Maybe this was daydreaming. Maybe it could never happen. But Mama was right when she said, "When you lie on the ground you can't fall very far." Surely, as far as money went, the Weiss family hadn't very far to fall. The boys and their sister were seldom really hungry. Ehrich had noticed, though, that Papa and Mama didn't eat as much as they used to.

"Take my dumpling, Ehrich," Mama would say. "I do not feel very hungry." Or Papa would say, "I have no taste for apple blintzes tonight. You boys divide mine amongst you. And mind you make the parts even." Mama didn't keep her cake cupboard locked any more. There was hardly ever a cake in it now.

As Ehrich walked down the dusty road he began to realize that, wherever he was going, there would be no Papa and Mama to see that he did not go to bed hungry, or to see that he went to bed at all, for that matter. There would be no older brothers to keep him from being teased about his queer clothes. Mama usually made them out of whatever the others had outgrown. There would be no Dash to tie him up with complicated knots and applaud when he got free.

He hadn't taken anything with him except a small piece of bread for his lunch. He didn't have an extra coat or pair of shoes. Papa had just patched the hole in the sole of one of his shoes last night. Ehrich could see him now, bent over the kitchen table in the lamplight, his long thin fingers working with the shoe and the cardboard. Papa shouldn't have to do things like that. He wouldn't, either, as soon as Ehrich became a magician. Papa was meant to be a scholar, as he had been in Hungary.

Ehrich was hungry almost before he'd left Appleton, but he made himself leave the bread in his pocket until the sun was straight overhead. He sat under a tree eating in small bites. If he made the bread last a long time, it would seem as if there was more of it.

When he'd swallowed the last bite he stood up and brushed the crumbs from the knees of his dusty brown suit. Any food he had from now on he would have to get for himself. Until now he hadn't thought very much about what it would be, or where it would come from.

It had been pleasant walking in the country in the spring morning. But Ehrich hardly saw the neat farms he passed. Instead he saw himself standing on a platform bowing. He would return home with presents for everyone.

By afternoon the day had begun to seem less pleasant. It was still chilly in spite of the sun. His feet hurt, especially the one with the mended shoe. He was thirsty. Once he decided to stop at a big white farmhouse for a drink of water, but an enormous black dog rushed at him, barking ferociously.

Now he couldn't seem to see the pictures of himself on the stage or coming back to Appleton with presents. Instead he saw pictures of the family gathered around the Sabbath Eve table or of Dash turning somersaults in the hall.

He had no idea how far he'd come. Perhaps he could still get back home before night. Perhaps that's what he should do. By this time his parents would know he was gone and would be really worried about him.

He'd been thinking so hard that he hadn't noticed he had come to a small town. He heard the whistle of an approaching train. It was a long freight heading down the track which ran squarely through the center of town. Shaking and grinding, it slowed and came to a stop. One of the cars was empty, and its doors were open. No one seemed to be looking at Ehrich.

He remembered how some of the boys in Appleton boasted about catching rides on trains. He had never mentioned this to his father. However, he was pretty sure what his father would have said. It would have been something about riding without paying the railroad company.

Still, there was an empty space on the train. And if he didn't get so far away he couldn't get back, he was afraid he would turn back right now. Then he would never be able to keep his promise to his father.

He could almost hear Papa's disapproving voice when, just as the train started to move, he jumped up through the door of the empty car and crawled into the farthest corner.

The train jerked along for a long time before it stopped again. Now Ehrich was sure he had gone too far to turn back. Cautiously he peered around the door. There was no one to be seen on this side of the train.

He jumped out, and there was a ripping sound. Now his long gray underwear showed through a three-cornered tear in his trousers. Holding the tear together with one hand, Ehrich looked about him. "Delavan" the faded sign on the small station said.

Judging by the sun, it must be late afternoon. Judging by his stomach, it might be tomorrow. Later he'd have to find a place to sleep. Now he would only worry about earning his dinner, and earning it right away.

He wasn't sure what he could do that anyone would pay money for. It didn't seem likely that anyone in Delavan would need anyone to walk a tightrope or pick up pins with his eyelids.

64

Neither was there anyone on the street needing a shoeshine even if he had anything to shine shoes with. He was pretty good at chopping firewood and bringing in water and other household chores. There was probably more work of that sort in the country than in town.

Tiredly he headed down the dusty road. He slowed down before each house he came to, trying to decide what kind of people lived there. He decided not to stop at a tall thin house with long, narrow windows. It looked like a frowning person with eyes set too close together. At the next house two little girls were sitting under a tree with their dolls. They stared at him and giggled, covering their mouths with their hands and whispering to each other.

He passed several more houses before he came to a small white one not too far back from the road. He walked slowly up the path and climbed the steps to the porch. He raised his hand to knock, but he couldn't do it. He felt like a beggar. Still, he was going to ask for work. That wasn't begging.

He didn't have to knock after all. The door opened, and a tall black-haired lady looked at him out of dark eyes, like Mama's. "What is it?" she asked in a low voice. She wasn't smiling, but she didn't look unfriendly.

"I need a job, ma'am," Ehrich blurted out. Then, when she didn't laugh or close the door in his face, he went on. "I need to earn my supper. I can chop wood or bring in water or—or anything you'd like to have done."

"Haven't you any home? Where do you live?"

"Oh yes, Ma'am. I have a home. But I don't live there anymore."

"I see." The dark eyes were looking at his shabby thin coat and torn trousers. "Suppose you come in and we will talk about it. My name is Mrs. Flitcroft. And you are?"

"Ehrich Weiss." Ehrich hadn't intended to use his real name, but those eyes were so much like Mama's that he could almost hear her saying, "Tell the truth and shame the devil."

He followed Mrs. Flitcroft through a cold bare hall into a big warm kitchen. Heat was coming from a black coal range. A kettle was bubbling furiously and smelling of beef and onions. Ehrich closed his eyes. He hadn't realized how cold, exhausted, and hungry he was.

"I'll tell you what," Mrs. Flitcroft said. "My stew is all ready to eat. Suppose I give you your supper now, and while you eat we'll talk about what you can do to earn it."

Actually Ehrich didn't talk much while he ate. He didn't know how many times Mrs. Flitcroft ladled more stew onto his plate or how many slabs of bread she spread with rich sweet butter. After he'd finished his apple pie she motioned him to sit in the rocking chair by the stove. She sat across from him in a straight high-backed chair, sewing.

Mrs. Flitcroft asked a few questions. Ehrich told her all about his family—about Appleton, about Jack Hoeffler's Five-Cent Circus. He even told her about his promise to Papa.

Suddenly he jerked his head up and blinked his eyes. How long had he been asleep? Was Mrs. Flitcroft waiting for him to answer a question? When he looked at her, she laughed and put her sewing down.

In the morning when he opened his eyes, sunlight was streaming into the room through a long narrow window by his bed. He barely remembered following Mrs. Flitcroft and her lamp into this small, white-walled bedroom last night. Now he saw his coat, neatly brushed, and his trousers, with the tear perfectly mended, on a chair by the bed. He sat up quickly.

"You look like a boy who's ready for eggs and

oatmeal," Mrs. Flitcroft said when she saw him standing in the kitchen doorway.

"But I haven't even earned my supper or my bed yet," Ehrich protested.

"Sit down at the table, Ehrich. I've been thinking about that. There really isn't much here that needs doing this morning. I think you should not waste time in starting to look for work." She slid an enormous bowl of oatmeal in front of him, poured cream over it out of a yellow pitcher, and passed the sugar.

"But I must pay you. I don't beg."

"Of course you do not beg. Anyone can see that. Sometime when you find a job, send me a letter and tell me what you are doing. That will be a payment."

Ehrich picked up his spoon. Some day he would do something for Mrs. Flitcroft—something nice she did not expect.

"One other thing, Ehrich," Mrs. Flitcroft said

as he ate his eggs and thick toast, "about your mother and father. I know you're trying to help them. But if I were your mother I could never sleep until I heard that you were well and that nothing had happened to you."

She handed him a postcard. "Please write to your mother. I will mail the card when I go to the post office this morning."

Ehrich stared at the blank card. Then he took the pencil Mrs. Flitcroft handed him and wrote slowly, "Dear Mama, I am going to Galveston, Texas. Be home in about a year. My best regards to all. Your truant son, Ehrich Weiss."

A Dollar a Week and Cakes

EHRICH searched through his pockets one more time. There was no reason to think there would be anything in them now when there had been nothing in them an hour ago.

Still, Mrs. Flitcroft had given him so much food that it didn't seem possible he could have eaten it all in one day. He had, though. There wasn't a crumb left.

He'd never been so hungry in his life. The sun was shining and the buds were swelling on the trees. But Ehrich couldn't think of anything but the hunger pain in his stomach.

Perhaps it was because he was so hungry that

he felt such a great longing for his mother and father in Appleton. Every time he thought of home he imagined it filled with tantalizing smells. Right now he could almost smell the sweet and sour tongue simmering in its sauce of onions, vinegar, and gingersnaps. And for dessert there might be apple strudel with its dough stretched so thin that you could read through it. He'd just have to stop at the next house and ask for something to eat.

He hadn't passed a house for miles, but once in a while he had seen a field where men were plowing deep furrows in the black soil. Maybe he could earn a meal by helping a farmer. There must be something a boy with willing feet and an empty stomach could do.

There was a small farmhouse at the top of the next hill. As he got closer he saw this was not a well-cared-for house. Its sagging gate swung carelessly in the warm breeze. A few scrawny chickens pecked lazily at the hard earth around the unpainted house. Slowly he walked up the broken steps and knocked at the door. A tired woman with untidy gray hair opened it.

"Please, ma'am, I wondered if you would let me do some work for a meal."

"Nothing around here needs doing." She slammed the door in his face.

Ehrich looked at the broken steps and the sagging gate. He would have thought there was a great deal which needed doing.

He had better luck at the next house. In the next few weeks he learned to guess pretty well where he would be given a chance to work and where he wouldn't. He chopped wood. He carried water to the men in the fields. He weeded gardens and cleaned out stables.

In small towns he delivered groceries and swept out stores. Sometimes he carried packages or watched baby carriages while mothers

74

shopped. He didn't starve, but he was a long way from having any money to send home.

He decided he might earn more money if he went East instead of to Texas. By June he had worked his way to Illinois. Sometimes he walked. Sometimes he rode on freight trains.

Late one hot afternoon he sat under a tree at the top of a hill. He had to decide whether to try for his next meal at the small town he could see at the foot of the hill or to follow the other road to a farm he could see in the distance. Usually he had better luck at farms.

He took his shoes off and wriggled his long toes. Then he stood up and looked down the hill again. What he had thought were houses down there were really tents. There was a small circus at the foot of the hill. Ehrich forgot about being tired. He put his shoes on and ran down the hill toward the circus.

Seeing a circus again was almost as good as

being home. He breathed in the wonderful circus air. For a few minutes he watched three rope men pounding stakes into the ground. One of them stood up and wiped his forehead with a dirty handkerchief. "You want something, kid?"

"Who do I ask about a job?"

Now all three men were looking at him. They laughed good-naturedly. "What do you do?" one of them asked.

"I am Ehrich the Great," Ehrich answered proudly. "I would like to talk to the head man and show him my act."

The rope man looked at the small, dusty figure. "Sorry, we didn't recognize you, sir. Mr. Walker is in the main tent. He's the manager. Talk to him."

Ehrich could hear them laughing as he walked away. Some day they wouldn't laugh. Then he heard loud angry words coming from the big tent. "You're a lazy good-for-nothing excuse for an acrobat. I'm tired of having to hunt for you before every show. Now get out of here before I throw you out. And don't come back."

A small wiry man scurried out of the tent opening, and Ehrich slipped quietly in. The manager was a tall man with red hair and a face to match. When he saw Ehrich he growled, "Well, did you deliver the handbills?"

"What handbills, sir?"

"Didn't I hire you to pass out bills?"

"No, sir, I'm Ehrich. Ehrich the Great." The Great Ehrich's voice sounded rather small and squeaky in the big tent.

The man scowled. "Ehrich the Great, eh? What next?" But Ehrich could see a small smile at the corners of his mouth.

"Yes, sir," he said quickly. "I came to show you my acts. I can walk a tightrope. Or I can do magic tricks. Or I can let anyone tie me up with ropes and I can get loose."

"Can you now?" the manager said. "Where was your last engagement?"

"With Jack Hoeffler's Five-Cent Circus, sir, in Wisconsin. I did a tightrope act there, but I'm better at rope escapes."

The manager looked surprised. "Well, we'll give it a try. If you're half as good as you think, we're both lucky." He opened the tent flap and called, "Hey, Joe, bring me a rope."

Joe was the rope man who had told Ehrich where to find the manager. When the manager told him to tie Ehrich up, he looped the rope carelessly around his chest and arms and tied three loose knots. He was still grinning.

Ehrich was scornful. "Really tie me up," he said, wriggling out of the rope and handing it back to Joe. Time after time Joe tied Ehrich up. Each time the knots were a little harder to untie, but each time Ehrich wriggled free.

At last the manager said, "All right, I'll hire

you just until I get another act. I'll give you a dollar a week and cakes."

A broad grin spread over Ehrich's face. He was glad he knew from working with the Five-Cent Circus that "cakes" meant meals.

Ehrich's act followed the trained dog act. Usually when Ehrich came into the ring the dog trainer was still trying to shoo his dogs out of the tent. Dogs were barking and the children were laughing and screaming.

Ehrich knew no one was paying much attention to him. "Someday," he thought, "I'm going to do something so they'll all be quiet and really look at me." He kept trying to think of some way to make his act more interesting.

"Mr. Walker," he said one day to the manager, "maybe when Joe ties me up the customers don't think he tries very hard. Why couldn't we ask somebody to come out of the audience and tie any kind of knots he wants to?"

"Are you sure you could get out of anything anybody could tie?"

Ehrich was indignant. "Of course I could."

The next night the audience was invited to tie Ehrich up. This time Ehrich had a little more applause than usual, but still not as much as he would have liked.

Mr. Walker had a hard time finding another acrobat, so Ehrich traveled with the circus through Illinois and into Indiana. He sent most of his money home. One hot August day the circus arrived in a little Indiana town.

At the evening performance, when Mr. Walker said as usual, "We challenge anyone to take this rope and tie Ehrich the Great so he cannot escape," the local constable stepped forward.

"It doesn't seem fair to use such a big rope to tie up such a little fellow," the constable said, "but here goes."

Ehrich had never been so well tied up before.

The constable wound the rope around and around him and tied ten or twelve tight knots. In five minutes Ehrich handed him the rope.

"You're a regular escape artist," the constable said. "How would you like to try getting out of these?" From his pocket he pulled a pair of shiny handcuffs.

Ehrich the Great hesitated a moment. Then he felt in his pocket with his fingers. His picklock was still there. "I'll try," he said, "if I can go off by myself."

"It's a trick!" someone jeered.

"There's only one way to get out of these cuffs," the constable said as he held up the key. "And as long as I have this in my hand, it will be a good trick if he can do it." The audience laughed.

Ehrich slipped behind the tiger's cage and began working with the piece of bent wire. In a very few minutes he stepped out from behind the cage. He was waving the handcuffs over his head. The audience cheered. The constable applauded the loudest of all.

After Ehrich had gone to bed that night he

went over his triumph again and again in his mind. At last the audience had really looked at him. The applause and the cheering had all been for him. Some day he'd have a better act and there would be bigger audiences.

Before the summer was over he received a letter from his mother. She told him that his father was going to New York, where he thought he might be able to support his family better. He hoped he would be able to send for the rest of the family soon. "Why don't you go to New York?" Mama wrote. "Maybe you could help."

It would be wonderful for the family to be together again. He'd start working his way toward New York.

A Place to Start

"OPEN YOUR EYES, MAMA. Look. You can see into stores, into people's kitchens even," Ehrich's voice coaxed. But Mama kept her eyes stubbornly closed. Her hands gripped the handles of the faded brown satchel she wouldn't let anybody else carry for her.

"Enjoy it, Mama. We won't be riding on the elevated train very often."

"A blessing indeed," Mama muttered. She leaned against Ehrich as the train picked up speed, swaying and jerking.

Ehrich and Rabbi Weiss had lived in New York almost a year by themselves before they could send for Mama and the others. Rabbi Weiss had the kind of school here he had tried to have in Appleton. Here on the East side of New York were many Jewish children. Ehrich helped with the school as much as he could, but since he knew no Hebrew he felt that his father might have managed as well without him.

Once in a while Ehrich made a little money as a messenger boy for some of the small businesses in the neighborhood. Every Friday he and his father counted their money. Every penny they could possibly spare went into a big black box. They counted the money in the box each week, too, even though they already knew exactly how much was in it.

At last one Friday, Papa looked at Ehrich with a smile. "There is enough," he announced. "Now we can bring Mama and Theo and Sister." Papa never would call Theo "Dash" as the rest of the family did.

Many letters in Papa's distinguished bold script and in Mama's spidery handwriting were sent. At last everything was arranged.

When the great day finally came, Rabbi Weiss decided that it was better for Ehrich to meet the family and bring them to the apartment. Ehrich was much quicker than his father at finding his way about the city.

This was partly because Rabbi Weiss did not read English as quickly as he read Hebrew or Greek. Also, when he rode on a horsecar or an elevated train, Papa always took a book out of his pocket. Sometimes he rode far past where he had intended to go.

"Don't be too proud to ask the way," his father had cautioned him when he left. "It's better to ask ten times than to go astray once." But Ehrich didn't need to ask too many questions. His errands as a messenger boy had taken him to many parts of New York.

He could never remember feeling happier than when he saw Mama's solid, black-clad figure through the crowd at the railroad station with Dash and Gladys beside her.

Mama held out her arms when she saw him. Her face glowed, but she shook her head. "Ehrich, how thin you are. You need good cooking."

Ehrich tried to hug them all at once. "And good cooking we'll have now," he said.

Ushering his family through the crowds and to the elevated train, he felt proud to be a real New Yorker. When Mama realized that they were to travel on a train high above the street, she refused to go. "I will travel only on the ground," she said firmly.

Ehrich was desperate. "But Mama, it's the only way to get where Papa is," he pleaded.

"We have feet," Mama answered. Her lips were set in a straight line.

"But Mama, you have no idea how far it is."

Mama stayed solidly planted on the platform. Passengers waiting for their trains stared at the little group curiously.

Suddenly Gladys sat down on the platform. "I'm tired," she announced.

"See, Mama? Gladys could never walk so far. And Papa's waiting for us. He'll be worried when we don't come."

Only the thought of Papa being worried moved Mama. Even then she changed her mind when the first train clattered noisily in, shaking the platform. Now she sat stiffly by Ehrich. Sister seemed to be feeling better. She and Dash sat in the seat behind, noisily pointing out the sights to each other.

"Look! Look at the policeman down there, riding on the horse."

"Look! A lady's hanging washing out way up there on her little porch."

"There's a boy making a face at us!"

"Make a face back."

"He's gone now."

But Mama steadfastly refused to look at anything until they were down on the sidewalk again. Then she didn't like what she saw. She frowned at the bits of paper and string and orange peel on the walk. "What kind of people live here that they should be so shiftless?"

"Mostly poor people," Ehrich said apologetically. He'd never really noticed how dirty the neighborhood looked.

Mama pushed an orange peel out of the way with her foot. Ehrich knew what she was going to say, and she did. "Poverty may come from God, but not dirt."

But Mama could find no fault with the cleanliness of the Weiss apartment. It was very small and very dark, but also very clean. The one window in the living room looked out on a brick wall. No sunlight ever shone through it except for a few minutes in the middle of the day when the sun was directly overhead. But it was as clean as Papa and Ehrich could make it.

The top of the little stove and the wooden drainboard of the sink were scrubbed, white. Ehrich looked at Mama anxiously as she stood in the kitchen doorway. Her dark eyes looked at the cracked plaster on the walls and the peeling brown linoleum on the floor. Then she looked at Ehrich and Papa and smiled. "It's clean," she said. "Now we must buy for supper. Such a goulash I will make."

Mama was very quiet when Ehrich took her out to the street where the market was. He was worried about what she would think about the noise and confusion. The street was lined with pushcarts. Boxes and barrels stood on the sidewalk. Everything was here in one cart or another. There were bread, fish, apples, tomatoes, onions—even jewelry, shoes, and woolen caps.

Crowds of people swarmed around the carts. Customers pinched and shook the food for sale. They laughed and argued about the prices and shook fists in one another's faces. Children raced through the crowd, chasing one another and screaming and running into people.

Ehrich needn't have worried about Mama. She was smiling. She went from cart to cart pinching tomatoes and arguing about the prices with the rest of the crowd. As they started home Ehrich said, "I was afraid you wouldn't like it. It's not like Appleton."

"No, not like Appleton," Mama said happily. "Till we came to America your papa and I were city people. Appleton was not right for us. Here we will be happy."

That night there was much happiness in the Weiss apartment. There was talk and laughter, and over everything the rich perfume of goulash simmering in its tomato sauce.

Ehrich had to give up his place in the one bedroom to Mama and Gladys, but he didn't mind. He and Dash slept on the parlor floor. It was good to wake up in the morning and see Dash's rounded face on the pillow next to his.

Dash woke up and saw Ehrich looking at him. He stretched and yawned. "Seems like the floors are harder in New York."

Ehrich grinned. "I don't mind. I like it. It'll toughen me up."

"What for?"

"For the time when I get back in show business again, that's what for."

"I heard Papa tell Mama you'd forgotten all about that," Dash declared.

"Well, I haven't. I don't worry Papa about it because he just doesn't understand. He thinks magic is just a game for a child. But I could make a living at it. I could even be famous like Dr. Lynn. I could——"

Dash yawned. Ehrich always got so excited. "All right," he said placidly. "It's all right with me. I like magic."

Ehrich began to feel more and more useless as a helper to Papa. Before Mama came, Papa had needed him as much for company as anything, but now he had Mama.

"Papa," he said one afternoon after Rabbi Weiss had dismissed school for the day, "don't you think it would be better if I found a job away from home? Every day there are jobs advertised in the paper. I could earn some money for us. I know I could."

Rabbi Weiss looked at his son for a moment. Then he sighed and nodded. "Yes, Ehrich," he said. "I think the time has come for you to go out into the city."

Ehrich had expected to get a job the first day. But everywhere he went, employers wanted someone older or someone with experience. It was almost a week before he ran up the steps of the apartment, three at a time.

"I'm a necktie cutter," he announced. "It's a real job, six days a week. The boss thinks I'm older than I am."

His father looked at him sharply. "And what would make them think that?" he asked.

But Dash interrupted. "What does a necktie cutter do?"

"He cuts neckties. That shouldn't be too hard to figure out."

"All day long? How could anyone like that?"

"It is possible to learn to like anything," his father said. "After all, even a worm in a jar of horseradish thinks its life is the sweetest in all the world."

"I don't exactly think that," Ehrich said. "I don't intend to be a necktie cutter all my life, but it's a place to start."

Ehrich the Great, Alias Cardo

THE BOYS CALLED, "Go to it, Ehrich."

"Run, boy, run!"

"You're almost at the wire."

As usual, Ehrich had won another race. The shouting came from the other members of the Pastime Athletic Club.

"Keep this up and you'll win the New York Junior Championship for us," the coach beamed. "But you've got to practice every day."

"I will, sir," Ehrich promised earnestly. "I intend to win that championship."

"He's always the first one up at home," Dash said, coming over to stand proudly near his

96

brother. "He runs a mile before breakfast every morning, rain or shine."

"That's what wins races," the coach agreed. "If the rest of you would get out before breakfast you might be champions, too."

In the crowded locker room Ehrich changed from running trunks to his old patched trousers. He folded the red satin shorts carefully. Mama had worked hard to make them from many small scraps Ehrich had brought home from his job as a tie cutter. Every night for several months, he had brought home three or four more red pieces for Mama to put into her big mending basket. What a night it had been when she finally showed him the finished shorts!

"See?" she had said. "I have often told you that bit by bit the plate is filled. Every night you brought three or four pieces. Soon there was enough for these."

Ehrich had thrown his strong, fifteen-year-old

97

arms around her until she gasped for breath.
"Thank you, Mama. I'll win so many races that
I'll be famous. I'll bring all my prize money to
you. You'll have to be satisfied with that until
something bigger comes along."

Mama shook her head. "Ehrich the Great again?" she laughed.

"You'll see, Mama." Ehrich was sure of the future, even if no one else was. He'd already given several magic shows for the Athletic Club. Now other clubs had heard of his skill and were asking him to perform for them.

His early interest in magic had been fanned into an intense blaze again by two of his friends. Jack Hayman worked next to him in the factory. Joe Rinn was captain of the track team at the Athletic Club. The two of them left Ehrich little time to think of anything but magic. Cards and silk handkerchiefs were cheap in the Bowery, and each new trick was shared.

"Hurry up, Dash," Ehrich urged as they started for home. "Ehrich the Great has an engagement to entertain the Friendly Circle tonight with his magnificent card tricks."

"I thought this was the night Cardo was supposed to hold the Literary Society of the Young Men's Hebrew Association spellbound."

Ehrich laughed. "When I have a chance to earn a dollar, I don't ever forget what name I use or where I'm going."

"Is Jack going to be your assistant?"

"Yes. And he told me he'd bought several new silk handkerchiefs to use in our grand finale," Ehrich answered eagerly.

"Then, Ehrich, please let me have the old ones," his brother begged.

"You know what Mama says. 'Don't pour out the dirty water before you have clean.' "

Then Ehrich smiled at Dash's disappointed face. "You know I'll give them to you. Then you can practice to be my assistant."

"Thanks, Ehrich." Dash smiled back. "Whew, it's hot! How about a quick swim before dinner? I'll race you to the river."

"Good idea," Ehrich agreed. He was an excellent swimmer. He would dive into the murky East River whenever possible. Even all the garbage floating in the water didn't bother him, since he and all the other boys in the neighborhood had learned to swim there.

The swim cooled the boys off so that the long walk home didn't seem as far as usual. They walked past rows of small Italian carts loaded with everything from rags to raisins. They passed two older men, stoop-shouldered and bearded. These men had the same scholarly look as Rabbi Weiss. Wearing black skullcaps and shawls, they were speaking quietly in Hebrew. They both nodded to the boys.

"America is supposed to be the melting pot of the world," Ehrich said suddenly.

"It is," Dash answered. "You can find Germans, Poles, Italians, Chinese, or any other nationality you want, all living within a few blocks of each other."

101

"That's what I mean," Ehrich argued. "They live here in America, but they don't melt. They all wear the same clothes they brought from their homelands. They all go on speaking their native languages. They eat the food they've been used to all their lives. They're still foreigners—not Americans."

"Give them time," Dash yawned.

"I guess you and I are more American than Papa and Mama," Ehrich went on. "Maybe it just takes a while."

"Why worry?" Dash asked, kicking a battered can along with his foot.

"I'm not, really. Come on, Dash, leave that can. I don't want to be late tonight. Jack taught me a new card trick. If we pull it off tonight I'm going to show it to Joe tomorrow. He'll never guess this one."

"Long live Ehrich the Great!" Dash laughed and hurried after his brother.

A Different
Kind of Key

"A WHOLE NICKEL wasted," Ehrich complained.
"This book isn't really about magic at all. It's
about some French magician named Houdin.
I'm not even going to read it."

"Money spent for a book is never wasted so
long as the book is read," his father said. "There
has seldom been a book written from which nothing could be learned."

Ehrich opened the book because his father
was watching him, but he didn't really intend
to read it. The man in the second-hand book
store saved books about magic for him. Whenever Ehrich had a nickel or a dime to spare,

103

he stopped by to see what the man had found. Next time he'd pay more attention to what the book was about.

He turned the pages slowly. Then he saw the words, "The lady will look as if she floats in the air." Excitedly he began reading.

The book told how the lady who looked as if she was floating on air was really resting on a hidden shelf. Robert Houdin must have been one of the greatest magicians who ever lived. Here in his books were the keys to things which had puzzled Ehrich for years. He went on reading long after Papa and Mama were in bed.

Houdin began one of his tricks by waving his wand over a little stick. Immediately the stick began growing until it became an orange tree which put out blossoms and then golden fruit. The book explained how this was done with little tubes managed by an assistant.

Houdin's most famous trick was performed for

King Louis Phillipe of France. He borrowed six silk handkerchiefs from ladies at the palace. Then he named several places where the king might choose to find them.

The king chose the foot of a small tree in the the palace garden. Houdin waved his hand through the air. The handkerchiefs vanished. "It is done," he announced. "Instruct someone to dig at the foot of the tree."

The king and his guests went out to the garden to watch the hole being dug. In a few moments the shovel struck a small iron chest. When it was opened the six handkerchiefs lay neatly folded inside. What happened was——

"Ehrich!" It was Mama. "You are up so early?" she said. Then she noticed his red eyes and his rumpled clothes. "Ehrich Weiss," she said crossly, "did you not go to bed at all? Have you been reading all night? How can you expect to do good work with no sleep?"

"I know, Mama." Ehrich knew she was right, but he wished she would stop talking so he could finish the book before he had to go to work.

All that week he had a hard time thinking of anything but Houdin and his book. "I know I could do some of the things Houdin did," he said to Jack. "He was really great. Even his name sounded great. Who's going to believe in a magician named Ehrich Weiss?"

Jack smiled. "There's nothing to stop you from using a different stage name," he said. "I think I read someplace that if you put an *i* on the end of something, it means *like*. You could put an *i* on the end of Houdin. Houdini—how's that for a magician's name?"

"Houdini. Houdini," Ehrich said. "That's it, Jack. And for a first name—let's see—Harold? Henry? Harry? That sounds good—Harry Houdini. Harry Houdini, the great magician. Someday you'll see that name in all the papers."

106

"Sure I will," Jack said, grinning. "In the meantime we'd better hurry up and get this batch of ties finished."

Ehrich didn't give up. "You're pretty good yourself, Jack," he said. "You don't want to cut neckties all your life. Why don't we quit and really go on the stage?"

"Not me," Jack said. "Magic may be more fun than cutting neckties, but it doesn't buy much bread and butter."

"You're as bad as my mother," Ehrich said. "She is always saying, 'If you have bread, why look for cake!' I say 'Why not?' We wouldn't have to quit our jobs right away. Maybe we could start by doing a longer act and getting better places to do it."

"Maybe," Jack said. "But right now here comes the foreman. Pick up your scissors."

Jack and Ehrich worked out more tricks. Dash spent hours with Ehrich on the roof of the tenement house, helping him with card tricks, rope escapes, and other magic.

One Sunday afternoon Papa and Mama came up to the roof while this was going on. "Such foolishness," Mama said. "A waste of strength."

"So long as it remains foolishness it is all right," Papa said. "It is when it becomes serious that it is a waste. But of course Ehrich knows that all this magic and playing with ropes is not a way to earn a living."

Ehrich's face was red as his long fingers worked on a stubborn knot. It was a good thing Papa didn't know what he was thinking. Or did he? You couldn't tell about Papa.

Jack and Ehrich called themselves the Houdini Brothers. Once or twice a week they put on a show somewhere. One day Jack said, "I'm quitting, Ehrich. You're like a slave driver, trying to make everything perfect. I just don't want to work that hard on magic."

Ehrich wasn't too disappointed. Jack was too easygoing to suit him. If Jack made a mistake, he would say, "Who'll know the difference in a hundred years?" Ehrich knew the difference today, and he wanted the act to be perfect. Anyway, he'd been thinking for several weeks that Dash could do as good a job as Jack, and then they'd really be the Houdini Brothers.

Dash had to be talked into being part of the act. He, too, thought Harry was a slave driver. But when he realized that he could keep half the money they earned, it sounded like a better idea. Only then did he agree to help.

The Houdini Brothers act wasn't too bad, but it wasn't too good, either. The boys always performed a few card tricks. Then Dash would fasten Ehrich into ropes and handcuffs from which he escaped easily. The audience always applauded politely, but Ehrich felt the way he used to at the circus—as if no one was really paying much attention. Usually some of them were even yawning before the show was over.

"We're not bad," Ehrich said to Dash one day, "but it just isn't enough. Too many people have this kind of an act. We need something bigger— something different."

The next day he went to a magic supply house. He had been there often before. The shopkeeper was always interested in Ehrich and his shows. "I know the very thing you want," he said. "It's the sack and trunk outfit."

"What's that?" Ehrich asked.

"It's a good trick for two people," the shopkeeper answered. "It's not hard to do, and it never fails to grab the audience."

"It must be pretty expensive," Ehrich said.

"As a matter of fact, the one I have is a pretty old one, and you're a good customer. How much money did you say you could spend?"

Quickly Ehrich added up what he had already

with what he could save if he went without lunch all the next week. "Five dollars, I guess." It wouldn't be enough, he was sure.

"Five dollars is just the price I had in mind," the shopkeeper said. "You'd better get your brother to help you carry it home."

The next week the Houdini Brothers tried out the trunk trick for the Friendly Society. The audience watched Dash tie Ehrich's hands behind his back, slip a heavy canvas bag over his body, and put him into the trunk. Then Dash moved a small screen in front of it.

In a few seconds Ehrich moved the screen aside and stood in front of the trunk, bowing and smiling. He opened it and showed the audience that Dash was now in the trunk, neatly tied up in the bag. Dash and Ehrich couldn't possibly have had time to change places, but somehow they had. This time the applause was more than polite. It sounded like music to Ehrich.

Exit Ehrich, Enter Harry

"LADIES AND GENTS, for only ten cents, you can see every sight. There on your right is Rosy O'Grady, the big fat lady. The dog-faced boy will give you all joy, and I'll show to you the boxing kangaroo. . . ."

The man chanting these words in front of Huber's Museum noticed that Ehrich had slowed down. "Come on in, young feller. There's a lot to see for a dime—the tenth part of a dollar."

Ehrich shook his head. "I've got to deliver these neckties," he said.

"You can see a lot in a few minutes—singing and dancing, magic acts."

113

Magic! Ehrich shifted the awkward bundle of ties to his other arm and searched in his pocket for a dime. Before he had time to think what his father would say about such a waste of money he was inside the museum.

It was really more like a small theater. On the stage a red-headed man was holding out his hands, which were handcuffed together. A pretty girl covered his hands with a bright green handkerchief. After five minutes the man triumphantly tossed the handkerchief aside, and the handcuffs clattered to the floor.

Everyone but Ehrich applauded. He was wildly excited. Here was a man earning his living at something which he, Ehrich, could do better. In a few minutes he was in the manager's office. The manager looked up from his desk.

"Yes?" he said coldly. This man would not be easy to convince. Ehrich looked down at the desk, biting his lip. There, as if by magic, lay a pair of handcuffs. Quickly Ehrich snatched them up and snapped them on his wrist. The manager glared at him.

"I don't know what you have in mind, young man," he said, "but the key to those cuffs has been lost for some time."

Ehrich turned his back and felt in his pocket. For a moment his heart sank. Then his fingers touched the tiny piece of metal he was looking for. In seconds he turned around, holding the open cuffs in his hand.

"Not bad," the manager said. "How soon could you begin work?"

"Just as soon as I deliver these ties," Ehrich said, grinning.

"Monday will do." The manager smiled for the first time. "What's your name, son?"

Ehrich hesitated a moment. Then he answered, "Houdini, sir. Harry Houdini."

Now "Harry" had three days to try to explain

to Papa and Mama what he had done, and why. He knew it wouldn't be easy, but it was even worse than he expected. "I don't want to be a necktie cutter all my life," he said over and over again during the weekend.

"But it's a steady job and you bring home money every week," Papa said. "You like this playing at being a magician, but who knows how long this job will last. One week? Two weeks? A month? Then what will you do?"

"Isn't having bread enough? Must you always look for cake?" Mama said, as he had known she would. He was sorry that he had to hurt her, but he knew he could make up for the worry he was causing her after he became famous.

"We can have bread and cake both, because I'm going to be the best magician in the world," he declared.

Papa shook his head. "Even if you talk from today until tomorrow, never will I believe this is the way for my son to earn a living. But you will soon be seventeen, Ehrich, and what you must do you must do."

It wasn't as much fun working at the museum as Ehrich had thought it would be. It was hard work. There were many shows a day, and Ehrich escaped from ropes as well as handcuffs at each show. Sometimes the audiences didn't seem to care very much whether he got loose or not. He became more and more discouraged as all his attempts to hold their interest failed.

"You're the best escape artist we've had," the manager said, "but there's one thing wrong with your act."

"What's that, Mr. Dexter?" Ehrich asked.

"You make it look too easy. The audience appreciates it more if they think you're having a hard time. Thrash around and let 'em think you're not going to make it. Then when you do, they'll really appreciate it."

Ehrich tried it at the next performance. The audience had never clapped so long before. A few of them even stamped their feet and whistled. Now he realized there was more to being a good performer than displaying his skills. He must also be a good actor.

There was something Ehrich had been wanting to do for a long time. Now he decided that if he didn't do it now he never would.

He had never forgotten Mrs. Flitcroft and the gift he wanted to send her in return for her kindness. He brought home only a few dollars from his first week's salary. The rest of the money he had spent for a silk blouse for Mrs. Flitcroft. He mailed it to her with a five dollar bill pinned to the collar.

He had thought Papa and Mama would be cross. But when he explained what he had done with his money, Mama nodded and said, "An unkept promise is a snake in the heart."

Ehrich's seventeenth birthday came a few weeks after he started work at Huber's. Mama prepared all his favorite dishes for dinner. "Presents we have not," she said, "but we have much love for you as always."

Ehrich said, "There is one present you could all give me, and it wouldn't cost a penny."

"That's the kind of present we can give," Dash said. "What is it?"

"Well, since I'm going to be Harry on the stage from now on, I thought perhaps I could be Harry at home, too."

"All right, Harry," Dash said. "One name is as good as another."

"Harry, Harry, Harry," Gladys chanted.

Ehrich looked at his father. "You haven't said anything."

"Silence is also speech," his father said. "This I cannot do."

"I guess I really didn't think you would,"

Ehrich said, "but everywhere else I'll be Harry from now on."

The next summer Harry left Huber's and went to Coney Island. There he wasn't paid. After each performance he passed a hat, and people put in whatever they thought the show was worth. After that he took jobs with one small show after another. He went as far as Kansas.

Rabbi Weiss was quite ill the next winter, and Harry spent as much time as he could in New York. One day his father called him into the bedroom. "Ehrich," he said feebly. "You must again make me a promise."

Harry took Papa's hand in his. It was so thin and white that he could almost see through it. "What is it, Papa?"

"I must know that you will always take good care of Mama."

"I promised you before, Papa."

"You were a boy then. Now you are a man."

"Can you believe, Papa, that I would ever not take care of Mama?"

"I know your intentions are good, Ehrich, but to do this you must settle down. There can be no more of this traveling over the country playing at magic."

Ehrich looked at his father and sighed. "I promise that I will do whatever is necessary to take care of Mama."

The next month Papa died. Now it was up to Harry to keep his promise. Perhaps he should give up being a magician and find a dull, safe six-day-a-week job. But no, he couldn't do that. He would have to keep his promise in his own way.

The Houdinis

"You will see that both of my hands are empty," Harry said. "Now I will light this candle. Watch closely, and remember that both of my hands are empty." Triumphantly Harry pulled a bright red handkerchief out of the candle flame.

Only two people applauded. The others strolled to the other side of the sideshow tent to find something more interesting to watch.

It was the summer of 1893. Harry and Dash had brought their act to the midway of the Columbian World's Exposition at Chicago. Their act was the same as it had always been, but here it was only one of hundreds.

123

People were more interested in the Eskimo or South Seas Villages or in seeing Little Egypt in the Streets of Cairo show. Even in the sideshow they seemed to prefer the Human Claw-Hammer to the Houdini Brothers. The Claw-Hammer would take a nail in his teeth, push it through a two-inch plank, and then pull it out again. This always got thunderous applause.

When the Exposition closed, Dash decided to go back to New York. "You can stay and starve if you want to," he said. "I'm going home."

"Don't go yet, Dash," Harry urged. "I read about a trick that'll really set 'em back on their heels. We'll try it tomorrow."

"All right, I'll stay one more day," Dash said, "but it had better be good."

The trick was good. Harry would borrow a watch from someone in the audience. Then he would apparently fall and break it. He would look dismayed and stuff the pieces into a pistol.

A target would be set up on Dash's head, and Harry would fire the pistol. Immediately a hidden spring pushed the unbroken watch up in front of the target. This act always brought enthusiastic applause and a sigh of relief from the owner of the watch.

One evening the show seemed to be going especially well, even before the watch trick. Harry's eyes shone. This was more like it.

Sometimes he had to ask several times for a watch, but tonight a gentleman on the front row obliged right away. Harry thanked him and slipped and fell as usual. As usual, a watch lay in small pieces where he had fallen. Harry looked at the pieces for a moment. "And now," he said, "my assistant will bring me a bag to put these pieces in."

Dash looked confused. Usually Harry left the pieces of the fake watch on the stage until after the performance. But Harry was hissing in his ear. "Hurry up. Get a bag. I broke the wrong watch. Keep smiling."

Dash managed a weak smile and gathered up the pieces in a small bag. They'd probably be arrested after the performance, he thought.

Harry was still talking as if nothing unusual had happened. "Now," he said, "we will put this bag of pieces in front of the target and see what happens when I fire my pistol."

Dash was as interested as the rest of the audience to see what would happen. Harry fired the pistol. Then he walked over to the target and peeked into the bag.

"Believe it or not, ladies and gentlemen," he said, "this watch is now just as it was when the gentleman handed it to me. If he will come back-stage after the performance, I will return it to him. And now for my next trick."

This time there was no applause. The watch owner was very angry, even when Harry promised to buy him a new watch. This took the Houdini Brothers' salary for the next two weeks.

Shortly after this, Dash left for New York. This time no amount of talking would persuade him to stay. Harry found a job at Kohl and Middleton's. This was a Chicago museum similar to Huber's where he had worked in New York. Here he did twenty shows a day for only twelve dollars a week. He kept his promise by sending most of the money home to his mother.

Admission to the museum was ten cents. For another ten cents the customers could go to the annex to watch a longer performance. Harry gave acts in both places. When he first came to Kohl and Middleton's, the featured performer was Horace Goldin, a well-known magician.

After one performance Harry squeezed into Mr. Goldin's tiny dressing room. "I'm Harry Houdini," he said, putting out his hand.

Mr. Goldin went on brushing rabbit hairs from his coat. "Harry who?" he asked, without bothering to turn around.

Harry's hand dropped to his side. "Harry Houdini," he said. "I'm a magician too."

Now Mr. Goldin looked at him out of hard

black eyes. "Well, what do you want me to do about it?" he asked.

"I thought, since we're both magicians we might be able to trade a trick or two."

Mr. Goldin laughed contemptuously. "Listen, kid," he said, "what do you mean trade tricks? I'm the headliner. You get twelve dollars a week and I get seventy-five. That makes me six times as important as you."

Harry was amazed. He had never thought of measuring a man by how much money he made. He hoped he never would.

Harry left Chicago and put on shows wherever he could find an audience. Sometimes his act consisted of magic tricks and sometimes of escape tricks. Gradually he worked his way east, and finally back to New York.

One spring afternoon he was hired to put on a show at a high school auditorium. He had started one of his standard tricks.

"See this glass of plain water? I will wave my wand over it and change it into ink."

As he waved the wand it caught the edge of the glass. The liquid splashed over the pink skirt of a girl in the front row. He'd been watching her all through the performance. He'd never seen such enormous dark eyes.

As soon as the show was over he hurried to find the girl before she could leave. The water in the glass had really been acid, and he hoped her dress wasn't spoiled.

When he tried to tell her so, her mother, who was with her, would not listen to the apology. "The dress is ruined," she said crossly, "and I've half a mind to have you arrested."

As she was being hurried out by her mother, the girl whispered to Harry, "Don't mind Mother. I thought you were wonderful."

Harry managed to find out that her name was Wilhemina Rahner. Two days later he rang the

130

bell of the Rahners' small white house. Mrs. Rahner came to the door. "What do you want? Are you up to more tricks?" she asked.

"Please, Mrs. Rahner," he said, "I would like to have another dress made for your daughter. If you will give me the ruined dress to get the proper size, I will replace it."

Ungraciously she gave Harry the dress. "Take it and be off with you," she said. Harry felt a little better when he saw Wilhemina waving to him from an upstairs window.

The next week Harry came back with an even prettier dress than the one he had spoiled. The Rahners need not know that he could never have paid for such a beautiful dress. Mama had worked all week to make it.

By the end of the summer the Houdinis were again doing an act. But this time it wasn't the Houdini Brothers. It was Mr. and Mrs. Harry Houdini who were amazing audiences.

"Things Will
Never Be So
Bad Again"

"WHO'S THERE?" a hoarse voice called through the cold rainy night.

"Harry and Bess Houdini," Harry answered. Tiny brown-eyed Mrs. Houdini had almost forgotten that her name used to be Wilhemina. "Wilhemina is too long a name for such a tiny girl," Harry had told her when they were first married. "I'm going to call you Bess."

Now Bess's head was bent against the howling wind as she followed her husband through the ankle-deep mud surrounding the Welsh Brothers' Circus. Somewhere ahead of them a faint light shone through the rain.

Now they could see that the light was coming from a freight car on a railroad siding. A big strong hand reached out and pulled Bess easily into the car. A large man with a walrus mustache beamed at them happily.

"I didn't know you were so young," he said, "but I'm glad to see you anyway. I'm Mr. Welsh. I wasn't fussy when I wired for a sideshow act. Just what is it you Houdinis do?"

"We do anything," Harry answered. "Our act is mostly magic though—a trunk escape, card tricks, mind reading, handcuff escapes. You name it and we'll do it."

"Well then," Mr. Welsh said cheerfully, "at the concert you can do some magic and your wife can sing and dance. Then you can do your trunk trick. Your wife can do mind reading, and the two of you can do the Punch and Judy show. You can work in your handcuff trick somewhere and of course you'll be in the parade."

Mr. Welsh pulled aside a flimsy curtain. Behind it was a space barely big enough for a narrow bunk and a straight-backed chair. "You'll sleep here," he said.

Then he added, almost as an afterthought, "The job pays twenty-five a week and cakes."

By this time heads were peering out from similar curtains all up and down the car. As soon as she and Harry were inside, Bess threw herself on the bunk and burst into tears.

"It's not that bad, Bess," Harry comforted her. "Someday we'll have a whole suite of rooms. We'll have the best of everything. You'll see."

Bess smiled shakily. "Of course we will. It's just that I'm so wet and tired. And two people couldn't possibly do all those things."

The next afternoon they found out that they could do all those things and more. A banner over an empty cage read "Wild Man from Borneo." Some rough-looking boys were stamping and calling out, "Where's your wild man? We've been cheated. We want our money back."

Mr. Welsh stood near the cage frowning. Harry slipped over to him. "Pull the cage out of sight and give me five minutes. You'll have your wild man," he promised.

In ten minutes the cage was pulled out by two frightened looking attendants. Inside was a savage creature with tousled hair. Its face was fierce, and it threw itself against the bars of the cage, growling ferociously. The customers were satisfied. This was the wildest looking wild man they had seen yet.

After that Harry was the wild man at every performance. He pretended to eat everything the customers threw into his cage, even lighted cigars and cigarettes. Not only did Harry not eat these gifts, he had no use for them at all. In all his life he was never to smoke. Endurance and lungpower were much too important to him.

The Houdinis worked frantically to make every penny they could. Bess sold sheet music by singing songs in the short time between shows. She was paid two dollars extra for fourteen performances. They managed to send twelve dollars back to New York every week.

The long hot summer days dragged on. They were exhausted. "Everything will be better soon," Harry kept telling Bess. "Things will never be so bad again." But he was wrong.

Soon after the circus closed for the season, they went to Nova Scotia with a vaudeville show. They worked harder than they had with the circus. They even helped put up posters and coaxed businessmen to buy extra tickets. But in spite of all their work the show was a failure. The manager deserted them, and the scenery and props had to be sold to meet debts.

Harry and Bess had no money to get back home. One night they slept in a hallway, where

136

Harry covered Bess with his coat. The next morning they persuaded the captain of the Boston boat to take them on board. They were to give a magic show to earn their fare.

But there was something they didn't know. Harry had never been on a boat before. As soon as it began to move he was desperately seasick.

"You simply can't give a show in another hour," Bess said, as she looked at her white-faced husband. He had been slumped miserably in a deck chair all afternoon.

"I will. I have to," Harry moaned.

He had set up the props when they first got on the boat. When the time came for the show he managed to stagger to his feet.

"Ladies and gentlemen," he began, with a glassy stare. Suddenly he pulled his handkerchief from his pocket and dashed from the room. Bess looked after him helplessly.

"I'm afraid my husband has been taken ill,"

she said in her small voice, "but I will entertain you. At least I will try."

She picked up a deck of cards. "If you will select a card," she said to a lady in the first row, "I will tell you—I mean, I will try to tell you, what card you have drawn."

After the card had been hidden, Bess looked at the deck intently for a moment. "Your card was the ace of spades," she said triumphantly.

"I'm sorry. It was the three of diamonds."

"I must have done something wrong," Bess said, her face reddening. "Let's try again."

Bess made two more wrong guesses. The third time the cards fell out of her small hands and slid in all directions over the slippery floor of the tiny lounge. By now the audience was trying hard not to laugh.

Bess picked up a match box from the small table in front of her. Taking a match from the box, she lighted a candle on the table. "Now I will pull a silk handkerchief from this candle flame," she announced hopefully.

She waved her hand over the flame. Suddenly there was a handkerchief in Bess's hand, but it was on fire. Several women screamed. Someone threw a pitcher of water over the candle, and Bess burst into tears.

A tall white-haired man stepped up to the platform. "Ladies and gentlemen," he said, "I have never seen anyone try more gallantly to help her husband. And you must admit that the show, though brief, was exciting."

The audience clapped. "I understand," the man went on, "that these young people are doing this show to earn passage money. Now I wonder if there isn't some way we could help."

In almost no time Bess was presented with a hatful of nickels, dimes, and quarters. Proudly she showed the gift to Harry and told him what had happened.

"It was awful," she said. "I was so ashamed. I hope I never have to do it again."

Harry hugged her. "You won't, Bess," he said. "You'll see. We'll get in a good show. Things will be better." But they weren't.

In a few weeks the Houdinis were stranded in St. Louis. It was bitterly cold. They had only a dollar and a half, which they spent for an unheated room. There was a black iron stove in the room, but since they had to provide the coal for heat, the stove stayed cold.

They were always hungry. Any food tasted good. One night Harry came home with six potatoes and some kindling wood. He wouldn't tell where the potatoes came from. The kindling was a packing case he had found in the street.

After they'd roasted the potatoes they sat comfortably by the stove. "It's the first time I've had warm feet and a full stomach at the same time since I can remember," Bess said.

"We've really hit bottom, Bess. Things are sure to be better now," Harry assured her.

Things were a little better after that. They worked for a few weeks in a St. Louis music hall. They traveled with a medicine show. They worked at the Welsh Brothers' Circus again. Then they went into business for themselves and played in both small and large towns.

At last they received a telegram from New York. An agent had booked them into Tony Pastor's theater, one of the best vaudeville houses in the country. "We've made it! I told you we would!" Harry lifted Bess off the floor in a crushing bear hug. "We're in big time now."

And they were, for a week. Their act was fairly successful, but at the end of the week they were back at Huber's Dime Museum.

That spring they were on their own again. Every time they came to a new town, Harry introduced himself to the chief of police.

"I am Harry Houdini, the Handcuff King," he would say. "I can escape from any pair of handcuffs you put on me." Usually the police were interested and would humor him. They were surprised at his quick escapes. Often the news would appear in the local paper.

When the Houdinis arrived in Chicago, Harry knew it would be harder to get his name in the paper. He asked some reporters whom he knew to introduce him to someone important at the city jail. In this way he met Andy Rohan, a detective lieutenant. He called on Mr. Rohan at the jail several times.

Then one day he announced, "I could escape if you handcuffed me and locked me in any cell in your jail."

Mr. Rohan was not too interested. The reporters urged him to let Harry try. They were looking for news stories. Rohan reluctantly put a pair of handcuffs on Harry's wrists.

142

Harry smiled. "Don't stop with one pair," he urged. "Put on two or three."

Shaking his head, Rohan put on two more pairs. Then he locked Harry in a cell. He and the reporters stayed in another room. In five minutes Harry walked into the room with all the open cuffs in his hand.

Instead of being impressed, the reporters all laughed. "We're not fools," they said. "Rohan told us you've been here twice before. It would have been easy to make an impression of the lock. You probably have a key in every pocket."

Harry's face was white. "Search me. Take away my clothes and put me in another cell," he said angrily.

In a few minutes he was locked up again, wearing nothing but three pairs of handcuffs. The reporters, who didn't like the idea of being fooled, had even taped his mouth shut.

Nobody laughed when Harry appeared

shortly, completely dressed. Pictures were taken. Stories appeared in all Chicago papers.

Bess was in bed in their rooming house, ill with the flu. She was almost too sick to care what happened.

That night Harry was called to the phone in the hall outside their room. The manager of one of Chicago's biggest theaters had called to offer the Houdinis a spot on his show that week.

Harry was desperate. Without Bess there would be no trunk trick, but he didn't want to admit to the manager that there was little else in the act. "Sorry," he said, "but I couldn't come unless I were the star of the show."

"All right," the manager said. "I'll give you star billing. I'll pay eighty-five dollars a week. Just come ahead."

Harry had never had eighty-five dollars all at once before in his life, but without Bess he couldn't accept. He swallowed. "Sorry," he said, "but I'd have to have more money." Surely this would end the offer.

The manager laughed. "You drive a hard bargain. I'll make it a hundred dollars."

"A hundred dollars!" Harry exclaimed.

At this Bess called out weakly, "For that money I'd work if I was dying. Tell him we'll take it before he changes his mind."

Being shown into the star dressing room was the best medicine Bess could have had. No one ever recovered from the flu so quickly. She and Harry never put on a better show in their lives, but at the end of the week they were back at the dime museum.

"We'll make it next time," Harry assured Bess. "And if not the next time the time after that, because I'm going to be famous. I know it."

Success Abroad

"YOUR ACT was rotten."

Harry's fingers shook as he set his cup down in its saucer. He hadn't expected this from the well-dressed stranger who had invited him and Bess to dinner after the show.

He opened his mouth, but their host held up his hand. "Just a minute. I said the act was rotten, but your escapes were great. You need to cut out the little magic stunts that any magician can do. Concentrate on the thrillers, acts your audiences haven't seen before."

Harry still wondered why this man thought he knew so much about magic acts until the stranger said casually, "I forgot to tell you my name. I'm Martin Beck."

Martin Beck! Harry glanced quickly at Bess. Martin Beck was one of the most famous showmen in the United States. He owned a chain of theaters and was known for paying well.

"I'll try you out at sixty dollars a week. If it goes well I'll raise it. Can you be in San Francisco by the first week in June?"

"I think so," Harry said. As usual, it was not time, but money which was lacking. In the next few weeks he and Bess managed to save enough from their small salary at the dime museum to pay their fares to San Francisco.

It would be cheaper to take their own food than to eat on the diner, they decided. Bess packed an enormous basket of chicken, biscuits, jam, and fruit. But the weather was hot. By the third day all the chicken had to be thrown away. They'd generously shared their fruit with the other passengers. By the time the train reached California, they had decided they never wanted to see biscuits and jam again.

Mr. Beck was right. Their new act was much better. Audiences liked them so well that their salary doubled. But when their contract ended in the fall of 1899, no one else hired them.

"I know what we need to do," Harry said one evening that spring. "We'll go to Europe and get famous. Theaters are always bringing in acts from Europe."

With Harry, to think was to act. By May they had scraped together enough money for the very cheapest passage, with just enough left over to last them a week in London.

LONDON

No one was much interested in hiring magicians in London either. Harry begged a young

149

theatrical agent to manage their act. The agent read the clippings about the Chicago handcuff escape thoughtfully.

"Now if you could escape from Scotland Yard handcuffs I wouldn't have any trouble signing you up," he said.

"Let's go," Harry answered.

"These aren't stage handcuffs, you know," Superintendent Melville warned him at Scotland Yard. "But if you insist, I'll show you how we take care of Yankees who come over here and get in trouble." He put Harry's arms around a big stone pillar and cuffed his hands together. "I'll come back for you in a couple of hours."

"Wait! I'll go with you." And Harry handed Superintendent Melville the cuffs and stepped away from the pillar.

This story spread all over London, and Harry soon had many offers from which to choose. On his opening night the theater was packed. Harry

had barely begun his act when a man leaped up on the stage. "I am the Great Cirnoc, the Original Handcuff King," he announced. His eyes were glittering. "Houdini is a fraud."

The audience was quiet, waiting to see what Houdini and the Great Cirnoc would do next.

"Get me the Bean Giant," Harry whispered to Bess. The Bean Giant was a handcuff invented by a Captain Bean of Boston. Captain Bean had offered five hundred dollars to anyone who could release himself from the cuff. Houdini had been able to free himself in a few minutes, but he had not received the prize because he refused to tell how he had done it.

Now he said to Cirnoc, "I will give you five hundred dollars if you can free yourself from this handcuff."

Cirnoc allowed himself to be fastened into the handcuffs. His face was red and his muscles were bulging. He struggled for several minutes before giving up. Houdini gave him the key, and even then he needed help to free himself.

Houdini challenged anyone to bring a pair of handcuffs from which he could not escape. The theater was packed every night for months. Harry could have stayed longer, but he had signed a contract to go to Berlin.

GERMANY

Houdini was an instant success in Germany. Long lines formed at the box offices. In one theater a wall was even knocked out so seats could be placed on the stage. His success in Germany was not hurt at all by the fact that he had learned to speak perfect German at home.

He had twice as many offers as he could fill. He decided to invite Dash to come over and share his success. He could do rope escapes almost as well as Harry already, and Harry could

153

teach him about German locks. He could accept the bookings Harry didn't have time for. And why not have Dash bring Mama? She could visit her old home, and see his success.

Before Mama and Dash came over, Harry spent a short time in London. There in a shop window he saw a dress which had been made for Queen Victoria. The queen had died in January of that year. "Queen Victoria was the same size as Mama," Harry said to himself in surprise. Impulsively he went into the shop.

"I'd like to buy that beautiful dress," he said.

When the shopkeeper had recovered from his shock he agreed to sell the dress. However, Harry had to promise that the dress would never be worn in England.

This was only a small part of Harry's plan. He took Mama to Budapest and arranged a party for her. He rented the glass-roofed palm garden, the finest hotel in Budapest.

When Mama saw the elegant room she shook her head and said, "A grand cage doesn't make a bird sing." Just the same she sat in a heavy gilded chair, wearing her new dress, and greeting her relatives like a queen.

Harry toured all of Europe triumphantly. Everywhere crowds cheered and stood in line to buy tickets. In Dresden he jumped from a river bridge handcuffed and emerged free in seconds. In Holland he was handcuffed to the arm of a windmill. The arm broke, but he was unhurt.

About this time Harry became furious with a German circus magician named Kleppini. Kleppini boasted at every performance that he and Houdini had once locked one another up in handcuffs. He had escaped easily, he said, while Houdini was helpess.

Harry decided to teach Kleppini a lesson. Wearing a false beard, he went to the circus where Kleppini was performing. When Kleppini started his usual speech he was surprised to see a bearded man leap to the stage.

"I am Houdini," the man announced. "I dare you to let me lock you up. Here are five thousand marks. They are yours if you escape."

Kleppini turned white. "Not today," he stammered. "It's not on the program. Perhaps some other time."

The crowd jeered. That evening Kleppini's manager called on Houdini to decide how the challenge would be carried out.

"May I see your cuffs?" he asked.

"Certainly," Houdini answered.

The manager picked up a complicated looking pair. "These are interesting."

"Those are French cuffs. They can be opened only by a combination of five letters."

"Oh, really. What letters open them?"

"You wouldn't tell Kleppini?"

"Certainly not."

"Well, the combination is C-L-E-F-S, the French word for keys."

The next evening Houdini brought a large selection of cuffs from which he invited Kleppini to choose. He quickly chose the French cuffs. "I will open these."

Houdini smiled and locked them on Kleppini's wrists. Kleppini disappeared into a small cabinet on the stage. "I will return in a few seconds," he said confidently.

More than two hours later Kleppini was still in the cabinet. The angry stage manager ordered the stage hands to pitch the cabinet off the stage with Kleppini still in it.

Houdini and the audience went home. Late that night Kleppini's wife came to beg Houdini to release her husband. He went back to the circus with her. Kleppini was sitting unhappily on the stage with his wrists held in front of him. The letters on the handcuffs still spelled CLEFS.

157

Houdini laughed. "I had a feeling your manager couldn't keep a secret. I changed the combination to an American word which means Kleppini—F-R-A-U-D." Kleppini was too angry to answer as the cuffs fell off.

After four years Harry felt that he had conquered Europe. He and Bess sailed for home, expecting to have more offers than they could handle. However, America still had no interest in Houdini. There were no offers. Disappointed and hurt, Harry and Bess went back to London.

"I'll never come back to America until they beg me," Harry vowed. At last, in January of 1905, he did receive a cable inviting him to perform at a leading theater in the United States at an almost unheard-of salary.

Proudly he cabled back that he was booked up solidly until the following fall. Then he would oblige them by coming back to America.

Success at Home

"LISTEN to that applause!" Bess caught Harry's arm as the red velvet curtain came down again. "It's even better than London."

Bess was right. It had taken fifteen years of hardships and hard work, but now the Houdinis were being paid twelve hundred dollars a week for the same act they had done for twelve dollars in the old dime museum days.

"We'll never need to worry again," Bess said happily. "We'll always have work."

"You're wrong, Bess. When we stop worrying, we're dead. If I can't keep my name in the headlines we won't last a year."

159

"But you can't keep your name in the head-lines all the time," Bess protested.

"I think I can," Harry replied.

He had great plans for the future. He would escape from such unbelievable places that the papers would be filled with his exploits.

He escaped from a coffin with the lid nailed down. He escaped from a sealed paper bag without tearing it. He was strapped and chained to a cannon to which a fifteen-minute fuse was attached. He freed himself from the cannon in six minutes and removed the fuse.

One of his most spectacular escapes took place in New York. His wrists and legs were fastened with padlocks. Then he was put into a packing box weighted down with two hundred pounds of lead. A steel band was fastened around the box and it was floated in the river at the end of one hundred feet of line.

Harry escaped from this one in fifty-seven

seconds. The nails and bands were still in place on the box. When, with some difficulty, these were pried off and the cover opened, the padlocks were in the bottom of the box.

Day after day the escapes went on. Harry kept himself in the headlines constantly. In the winter he broke out of jails. In the summer he leaped handcuffed from bridges.

In Boston he was locked in a cell on the second tier of the city jail. His clothes were locked in a cell on the first tier. After he had been locked in, several reporters waited in the superintendent's office. In exactly twenty-three minutes the phone rang.

"You're where?" the superintendent asked.

"You what?" His voice was frantic.

He hung up the phone. "Guard! Guard!" he called. "Hurry! The prisoners have escaped! This is an emergency."

"Can't talk to you now," he told the reporters

as he started to the door. "Houdini called and said he let all the prisoners out."

A guard came running in. "It's all right, sir. He locked them all up again, only he put them in different cells."

It was true. Houdini had unlocked his cell, recovered his clothes from their locked cell, released the prisoners and locked them in other cells. Then he managed to open two locked steel doors into the prison courtyard.

He scaled the high wall and jumped into his waiting automobile This had taken him sixteen minutes. He had spent the other seven minutes getting to the theater.

He accepted all sorts of impossible challenges. Many of them were very dangerous. In Los Angeles his fans dared him to be buried alive under six feet of earth.

He worked out his plan for this carefully ahead of time, as he always did. One day he had himself buried under one foot of earth. He escaped easily from this. The next day he was buried under two feet of earth. He went on increasing the depth each day. When he reached the four-foot level it was almost too much for him. But he insisted on going ahead.

On the day of the challenge he felt less confident than he looked when he peered into the deep hole. But he jumped down quickly. Covering his head with a black hood, he motioned that he was ready for the hole to be filled.

As the dirt covered him he bent over so there would be an air space beneath him. Frantically he began digging. Then he forced himself to slow down. The one thing he must not do was to panic. Again and again he had to slow himself down until at last one hand pushed through to the air, and then his head and shoulders. He took deep breaths of air. This was a stunt he never chose to repeat.

Just when it seemed as if Houdini could not possibly outdo his former escapes, he always thought of something even more daring. "I've got it, Bess," Harry said one day. "I have an idea for a strait jacket escape."

"That's nice, dear," Bess said absently. But even she was worried when he told her he intended performing this escape while hanging upside down several stories above the street.

Bess knew better than to argue. In a few weeks five thousand people stood in the street watching Houdini. He hung upside down from the Kansas City Post building, laced in a canvas and leather strait jacket.

These jackets were used at that time to prevent mentally ill people from hurting themselves and others. The patient's arms were crossed in front of him. Then the long sleeves, which covered his hands, were tightly tied, pulled to the back, and buckled firmly. It was thought that it was impossible to escape from a strait jacket. Houdini had escaped from them before, but only on the stage. Now he was hung by his ankles thirty feet above the street.

His body doubled up and swung from side to side. Not a sound came from the crowd as they watched the struggling man. There were wild cheers when Houdini suddenly jerked the jacket over his head and tossed it into the crowd. It had taken him just two and a half minutes.

The great milk can escape was a trick which packed theaters night after night. Two attendants would bring an enormous milk can on stage. The audience watched them fill it to the top with buckets of water.

Then Houdini came in wearing a bathing suit. "Ladies and gentlemen," he would say, "I invite you to join me in a contest. I am going to lower myself into the can without the lid and stay under water for just one minute. If you are in good physical condition you might like to try holding your breath with me. A minute may be longer than you think."

Houdini jumped in with a mighty splash. The audience was quiet as most of them tried to hold their breaths. Ten seconds. All was well. Twenty seconds. Faces were beginning to turn red. Forty seconds. By this time most of the audience had given up.

Houdini emerged when the minute was up, dripping wet and not even breathing hard. "Now," he said, "the lid will be fastened tightly to remain so until I escape. As you can imagine, this will take much longer than one minute. If I do not escape within a certain time my assistants, who are standing by with axes, will smash the can and try to save my life."

This time after Houdini crouched in the can, the lid was padlocked tightly while a committee from the audience came to the stage to watch.

A small cabinet was lifted over the can. The orchestra played "Asleep in the Deep."

One minute. Two minutes. The audience remembered how long one minute had seemed. Three minutes. Why didn't the attendants use their axes? Three and a half minutes. The curtains parted and Houdini stood in front of the can. Water streamed over the canvas on the stage. The locks were still in place on the lid of the milk can.

Houdini felt that the most dangerous escapes he made were from locked safes. A safe had little breathing space. If he made a mistake and jammed the lock it would be necessary to dynamite the safe to get him out.

Unfortunately a safe escape did not look particularly dangerous, so it called for showmanship. Usually the audience suffered with Houdini for forty-five minutes before he appeared in front of the screen around the safe. His face would be shiny with perspiration, and his bushy hair would be standing up wildly around his face. For the last fifteen minutes people would have been calling for someone to break open the safe and rescue Houdini.

Actually the escape took him only two or three minutes. If he appeared that soon, people would have thought this was not worth watching. Therefore Houdini had spent the rest of the time sitting behind the screen, usually reading a book about magic. When he felt the audience was worried enough, he would muss up his hair and appear in front of the screen, looking hot and exhausted. As a matter of fact, the audience was much more tired than he was.

One of the successes Houdini enjoyed the most took place a long way from the stage. One week he said to the manager of the theater where he was playing, "I would like to have my salary paid in gold this week."

"Did you say gold?"

"I said gold," Harry said firmly.

After the astonished manager had visited several banks to round up a thousand dollars in gold pieces, Harry hurried to his mother's flat.

"Hold out your apron, Mama," he ordered. "It's for you," he told her as he poured the golden stream into her lap. Her eyes shone as he had known they would when he was a boy.

Many people insisted that Houdini must have some special powers. However, he always laughed at this idea. Everything he was able to do was the result of much careful study and planning and physical training.

In spite of the many dangerous things he did Harry Houdini was really most cautious. He practiced each tiny detail over and over. Even when the Houdinis were entertaining guests Harry practiced. Bess was quite used to the sight of Harry with his shoes off, tying and untying knots in a piece of rope with his bare toes. But guests were usually quite surprised.

Even the bathtub at the Houdini home served two purposes. It was large enough for Houdini to submerge completely. Here he practiced holding his breath under water. Bess timed him with a stopwatch each day. He could go without breathing for as long as four minutes. Often he practiced with huge chunks of ice in the tub. This conditioned him for jumping into icy rivers.

Fortunately Houdini required less sleep than most people. Five hours of sleep a night left him feeling fit and ready to run several miles before breakfast, which he did every morning. He said that by sleeping only five hours he gained three extra hours a day. This gave him more than a thousand extra hours a year to study and exercise while others were asleep.

Every day he practiced slow breathing exercises for hours. This helped him learn to use

171

as little oxygen as possible when he was sealed into an airtight container.

Houdini knew something about every kind of lock ever made. He needed only a tiny wire for a picklock to escape from any handcuff.

His jail escapes also required some sort of picklock. Houdini was always thoroughly searched and led into his cell wearing no clothes. However, he said, "I always had a picklock."

Sometimes he was able to shift the pick from one place to another while he was being searched. Once he even managed to slip it under the collar of one of the searchers and retrieve it as the man left the cell. At other times he was able to hide a pick ahead of time either in the cell or on the floor or wall just outside, where it could be easily reached later.

Often he used specially constructed equipment. In all his escapes from boxes, confederates had been able to replace the nails in one end

172

of the box with short nails. This made it possible for Houdini to push the board out with an elbow and replace it once he was out. A committee from the audience always inspected the box, but they usually spent their time looking at the chains and padlocks around it.

The sealed coffin from which he escaped had been made with short screws holding the bottom to the top. This coffin was very heavy, but Houdini, on his hands and knees, arched his back and lifted it by sheer strength.

The strait jacket escape was also done by muscular control. When he was fastened into the jacket he stiffened his arms. When he relaxed them, this gave him a little extra room.

Using only strength and persistence, he managed to work the sleeves first over one shoulder and then over his head. He worked at strengthening his fingers so that he could unfasten the buckles through the heavy canvas.

As for the milk can, it was cleverly constructed so that the entire top lifted off, padlocks and all. Also, he always jumped into the can with as great a splash as possible. Every drop of water which he managed to splash out of the can left that much more air space inside.

The curtained cabinet in which he performed many of his escapes held many secrets. A pick-lock was concealed in the leg of a chair. If necessary he could twist his body so that he could hold his handcuffs against the pick.

These secrets, however, played only a small part in Houdini's success. Most important were his physical strength, his knowledge of locks, his planning of every small detail, and his great courage.

New Challenges

"My next trick will be 'Money for Nothing.'" Houdini flipped a gold coin toward the audience and into a soldier's lap. Soon the soldiers were all standing and cheering as coin after coin flew through the air.

It was 1917, and Houdini was using his skill to entertain the soldiers of World War I. He had been furious when he was turned down by recruiting officers as being "too old" to serve in the army. Surely no recruit of half his age was in better physical condition. Houdini did not think that anything the army could do would be too much for a man who could jump handcuffed into an icy river or hang by his heels from a three-story building.

Since he could not serve in the army, Houdini spent much of his time and money entertaining the troops. Before the war was over he had given away thousands of dollars worth of five-dollar gold pieces in his mysterious "Money for Nothing" trick.

He appeared tirelessly at hundreds of bond rallies, where he sold a million dollars worth of Liberty Bonds to help pay for the war. Using his knowledge of escapes, he invented a diving suit from which a diver in trouble could release himself safely. He presented the plans for this under-water suit to the navy.

A NEW CAREER

"Those stupid pilots are too close. They'll crash, and Houdini will be killed before the end of the first reel." The camera man in the third plane kept cranking his camera in spite of his grim prediction.

Houdini was balanced shakily on the wing tip of one of the clumsy biplanes. His knees were bent. In about ten seconds he could jump to the other plane. Nine . . . eight . . . seven . . . It was coming too fast. Houdini braced himself. There was a grinding noise, and the wings of the two planes touched. He tried frantically to scramble back into the cockpit as both planes spiraled toward the ground.

"They're crashing. I knew it!" the camera man cried. "No, they're pulling out of it, but they're landing in the swamp."

"Can you see Houdini?" the pilot asked.

"No, but he couldn't possibly be alive."

But Houdini was used to being alive when he couldn't possibly be. In a few minutes he was rising out of the mud like a swamp creature.

It was 1919, and Houdini was starting what he thought would be a new career. He was one of the few actors who felt that the new film industry would replace stage shows such as his.

This was Houdini's second movie. His first one was a serial called *The Master Mystery*. In those early days of the movies, serials were popular. These were long, exciting stories, only one chapter of which was shown each week. Every chapter ended with the hero in some horrible situation. The serial fans would come back the next Saturday to see how he got out of it.

Houdini was tied up with barbed wire while a river of acid crept toward him. He was tied up with ropes under an elevator which was coming down slowly to crush him. He was nailed into a packing case and thrown into the ocean. And all this happened in just three of the thirteen chapers in *The Master Mystery*.

This serial was probably the first monster

picture. The evil monster, made of steel, lurched out of his secret hiding place at least once in every chapter to threaten Houdini's life in some fiendish way. Houdini in this picture was Quentin Locke, a secret agent of the Department of Justice. In the last chapter, of course, he triumphed over the monster.

Thousands of boys all over the country watched Houdini's rope escapes in chapter after chapter. Thousands of mothers all over the country wondered what had happened to their clotheslines.

The director of the picture wanted Houdini to use a stunt man for the most dangerous deeds, but he refused. "Who could you get that could do it better than I can?" he asked.

Houdini found a new interest while he was in Hollywood. This was the first time in twenty-five years he and Bess had been in the same place for more than a few weeks at a time. Soon his dressing room was full of clippings, old programs, papers, and books.

He had begun writing a book about the sideshows of the old dime museum days. He wrote about the fire-eaters and sword-swallowers who had made the sideshows so exciting. This was the first of a number of books which he was to write about magicians.

In 1921 Houdini formed his own film company, the Houdini Picture Corporation. Always sure of his abilities, he decided that he could write the script, supervise the photography, be the star and director, write the titles, and take care of the publicity. Dash gave up his own show to take over the business details.

Their first picture was *The Man from Beyond*. It was the story of a man who was frozen into a block of ice and chopped loose alive a hundred years later. The whole story was written by Houdini in ten days.

180

The biggest scene in the picture took place on the brink of Niagara Falls. Here Houdini rescued the heroine, whose canoe had plunged over the falls. This was the best part of the picture, the only good part according to most of the people who saw it.

Both this and another picture Houdini made were anything but successful. He tried to coax people into the theaters by putting on stage shows. At this time he performed one of his most famous illusions—making an enormous elephant disappear.

An elephant was led onto the huge stage of the Hippodrome. A tank of water under the stage made it impossible to use a trap door in the trick. The great beast stepped into a cabinet and curtains were drawn around him. When they were opened again, he was gone. "Even the elephant doesn't know how it was done," Houdini always "explained."

Even the vanishing elephant, however, could not hide the fact that Houdini was a better magician than he was an actor. This was the end of his career in films.

BACK OF THE BEYOND

One thing troubled Houdini very much. Many people whose relatives have died hope to hear from them again. After his own mother died, Houdini became interested in this and thought it might be possible.

A medium is a person who tries to receive messages from people who have died. Some of the mediums were sincere. Most of them, however, were frauds, and this made Houdini very angry. He did not like to see tricks played on people who were sad already.

Most of the messages were received during meetings called seances. A seance, which was held in the dark, could be very impressive. Furniture moved all by itself, ghostly voices were heard, bells rang, and trumpets played. Usually the medium would be holding the hands of other people at the seance to show that she had nothing to do with the things which were happening. Then she would repeat the messages she said she was receiving from the spirits.

Houdini went to many of these seances. At first he hoped to hear from his mother. However, his magician's eye could easily see that most of the mediums were using magician's tricks.

Houdini began sending people to seances to help him prove his suspicions. Sometimes he would send an unmarried woman to ask for a message from her dead husband. The medium would usually oblige by giving one to her.

Often he made his own investigations. Being Houdini, he liked to be as dramatic as possible. One evening he appeared at a seance wearing a white wig and beard. Houdini never did anything by halves. He tottered when he walked. His voice shook pitifully when he asked the medium for a message from his dead son.

The medium took his money and told him she would try to get in touch with his son. She and Houdini and the others at the seance sat in a circle touching hands. It was quiet for a few minutes. Then a shining trumpet arose from a dark corner of the room and began to play all by itself. Everyone gasped.

Suddenly a powerful flashlight was pointed toward the trumpet. Now they could all see that a man dressed all in black was holding the trumpet to his lips with black-gloved hands. The feeble old man was tearing off his beard. "It is I, the great Houdini," he said. "I hereby accuse you of fraud and deception."

Sometimes this feeble old man appeared at a seance with a hump on his back. This not only made him appear more pathetic, but it had a practical purpose. It concealed a camera which Houdini put to good use.

Houdini often staged seances himself to show how mediums achieved some of their ghostly effects. Even though the guests at one of Houdini's seances knew that everything they would see would be a trick, they were still startled at the spine-chilling things which happened.

When everything was quiet and dark, a glowing ghostly figure would drift into the room through a window. Head downward, it would float through the air, walk upside down on the ceiling to the other side of the room and vanish through another window. Some of the guests had even felt a ghostly hand brush lightly against their faces.

"It's just a trick," Houdini would assure his shivering visitors. They could hardly believe it.

In the darkness the guests had not seen a

black-clad figure slip into the room in stockinged feet. This figure was a trained acrobat hired for the occasion. He tiptoed across the room to the window and helped a fellow acrobat through it. The second acrobat's clothing was lightly sprayed with luminous paint. By doing a hand-stand on the first acrobat, it was easy for him to walk across the ceiling and disappear through another window on the far side of the room.

Mediums and seances were becoming more and more popular. Houdini wished there was a way to show larger numbers of people how easy it was for them to be deceived. Perhaps there was. Why not hold fake seances on the stage?

With Houdini, to think was to act. Soon a fake seance was part of each one of his shows. These seances were very popular. They were even attended by mediums who wanted to see what he would do next.

At a fake seance Houdini would ask for volun-

teers from the audience. Then he put black velvet hoods over their heads, explaining that this was how things would look to them in a medium's dark seance room.

He sat down with them at a table, facing the audience. They all held hands. Those sitting next to Houdini were told to hold their feet firmly against his to be sure he did not move from his place.

Soon the table in front of them began to rock back and forth. Bells sounded and tambourines played. The volunteers could feel various objects floating back and forth over their heads. Some of them even felt their chairs being jerked up and down.

The people on the stage were sure that Houdini had nothing to do with all these things. After all, they were holding his hands and touching his feet. The audience, however, had a better view of Houdini. They could see him quietly slip his feet out of his shoes and with his toes make the table move, the bells ring, and the tambourines shake violently.

One of the most baffling things which happened during the stage seances was spirit writing. Houdini invited one of the men on the stage to write a question on a slate. This slate was covered with another one, and the two were tied together so that Houdini could not see what had been written. Together the writer and Houdini held the slates under the table. The scratching of a ghostly pencil could be plainly heard. When the slates were opened, the question had been mysteriously replaced by a more or less sensible answer.

Houdini said he could duplicate on the stage any effect produced at a seance, and he never failed. He felt that if he had been able to keep anyone from being cheated by a false medium, this would be his greatest achievement.

Houdini was extremely generous, especially toward children and old people. He was always quiet about his generosity. It was not until after his death that it was discovered that he was completely supporting a number of old people. Many of them he had never even met. Once when he was asked why he did all these things so quietly, he said, "You don't hire a band every time you do a favor."

One winter when he was performing in Edinburgh, Scotland, he noticed that, although it was very cold, many of the children wore no shoes. He bought three hundred pairs and announced that he would give a pair to any shoeless child in Edinburgh. There was a wild scene after the show as actors tried to fit the three hundred pairs of shoes to a sea of children.

After all the shoes had been given out, there were a number of disappointed children left.

Houdini marched every one of them to a boot-maker's shop and saw that each of them had a pair of shoes. He and Bess had to watch their expenses for a time, but they were used to this.

Often he invited everyone in some old people's home to attend a performance free of charge. He also performed free of charge at many prisons. Perhaps this audience, more than any other, appreciated his skill at picking locks.

He never forgot his experience with the haughty magician in Chicago. Many times he went out of his way to encourage some struggling young magician whom he liked.

Not many people have the distinction of having their names accepted as part of the language. At the height of Houdini's success a new dictionary carried the word "houdnize." It meant, the dictionary said, "to release or extricate oneself, as by wriggling out."

And wriggle out he did—out of jail cells and

191

bank vaults, leg irons and handcuffs, padlocked boxes and air-tight coffins let down into deep water, sealed mailbags and tight strait jackets. Houdini was even "seen" to walk through a real brick wall. This wall was ten feet long and twelve inches thick, and it was built on the stage as the audience watched.

Houdini was once told that his courage must be his main source of power. "It is," he admitted, "and I must practice it as often as I practice my card tricks."

Here was one magician who did not suffer the gradual fading of his popularity which is so painful for entertainers. He continued to remain in great demand until the day of his death at the age of fifty-two.